Young Person's Guide to the

GLOBAL CRISIS

and the alternative

For my grandchildren

Young Person's Guide to the

GLOBAL CRISIS

and the alternative

Michael Barratt Brown

SPOKESMAN
for
Independent Labour Network

Acknowledgements

I owe the original idea of this book and many ideas for its presentation to my grandson, Elliot Ronald. If I didn't adopt them all, that is my fault and not his. John Hughes read an early draft and offered valuable comments. Ken Coates read each draft as it was written and gave much encouragement as well as many important suggestions. Tony Simpson and Jeff Goatcher saw the book through the press with exemplary care and concern. Illustrative graphs and pictures have been included, some of them from The Economist, The Guardian, *and the* Financial Times, *to whom grateful acknowledgements are given. A list of sources is given at the end of the book.*

First published in 1999 by
Spokesman
Bertrand Russell House
Gamble Street
Nottingham, England
Tel. 0115 9708318
Fax. 0115 9420433

Publication list on request

British Libraries Cataloguing in Publication Data available on request from the British Library.

ISBN 0-85124-620 6

Printed by the Russell Press Ltd. Tel: (0115) 978 4505.

Contents

List of Boxes

"Even in such a time of madness as the late twenties, a great many men in Wall Street remained quite sane. But they also remained very quiet. The sense of responsibility in the financial community as a whole is not small. It is nearly nil. Perhaps this is inherent. In a community where the primary concern is making money, one of the necessary rules is to live and let live. To speak out against madness may be to ruin those who have succumbed to it. So the wise in Wall Street are nearly always silent. The foolish have the field to themselves. None rebukes them. There is always the fear, moreover, that even needful self-criticism may be an excuse for government intervention. That is the ultimate horror.

So someday, no one can tell when, there will be another speculative climax and crash. There is no chance that, as the market moves to the brink, those involved will see the nature of their illusion as so protect themselves and the system. The mad cannot communicate their madness; they cannot perceive it and resolve to be sane."

"Throughout the twenties production and productivity per worker grew steadily between 1919 and 1929, output per worker in manufacturing industries increased by about 43%. Wages, salaries and prices all remained comparatively stable, or in any case underwent no comparable increase. Accordingly, costs fell and with prices the same, profits increased. These profits sustained the spending of the well-to-do, and they also nourished at least some of the expectations behind the stock market boom. Most of all they encouraged a very high level of capital investment . . . A large and increasing investment in capital goods was, in other words, a principle device by which the profits were being spent. It follows that anything that interrupted the investment outlays anything, indeed, which kept them from showing the necessary rate of increase – could cause trouble. When this occurred, compensation through an increase in consumer spending could not automatically be expected."

"In 1929 the rich were indubitably rich. The figures are not entirely satisfactory, but it seems certain that the five per cent of the population with the highest incomes in that year received approximately one third of all personal income. The proportion of personal income received in the form of interest, dividends and rents – the income broadly speaking of the well-to-do – was about twice as great as in the years following the Second World War.

This highly unequal income distribution meant that the economy was dependent on a high level of investment or on a high level of luxury consumer spending or both. The rich cannot buy great quantities of bread. If they are to dispose of what they receive it must be on luxuries or by way of investment in new plants and new projects. Both investment and luxury spending are subject, inevitably, to more erratic influences and to wider fluctuations than the bread and rent outlays of the $25-week workman."

John Kenneth Galbraith, The Great Crash 1929, *Pelican Books Edition, 1962, pp.20-21, pp.192-193 and pp. 194-195.*

Introduction

Why this book?

This book is aimed at young people – in sixth forms, at universities and colleges, in their first jobs or still looking for a job. It's about crisis in the global economy, which seems pretty much of a turn off, but it has become important, because getting jobs and keeping jobs depend on what is happening to it; and a whole generation could be blighted by it, like the generation that came to the job market in the 1930s.

Job losses from factories closing in the north of England and down-sizing in the Midlands have now reached even into the heart of the City of London, and when the smart burger bars like Deals and London's Fashion go bust and London International, the world's largest maker of condoms, loses money, something must be very wrong.

Young people are asking those of us who can remember the last slump in the 1930s, what happened then and why it should happen again, after 50 or 60 years with no big slumps since then, only some recessions – and a World War. The book should also be useful for the not-so-young, who also want to know what is happening to jobs and money, their mortgages and pensions, in the current crisis.

This book tries to answer these questions, but as they are economic questions, the answers have to use some economic language. To help with the jargon, there is a glossary at the end of the book, which can be torn out and used as a book mark, for reference when a new technical term turns up.

As far as possible, complicated economic concepts are avoided. Statistical tables and graphs have been included only as illustrations. There are a lot of figures in the book, some of them pretty astronomical, measuring incomes in millions and billions, even trillions. But any one who follows football players' transfer fees or "Countdown", and can estimate the salary of Ms. Vorderman, should have no trouble.

On the other side of the jargon divide, some economists will be irritated by the simplifications, not to mention the rejection in the book of much that goes for conventional wisdom, which, for example, saw the new German Finance Minister, Oskar Lafontaine, a moderate follower of Lord Keynes, as "the most dangerous man in Europe".

Keynes is here given his proper place as a wise guide to managing a capitalist system so as to avoid slumps, and Marx too is quoted as the most powerful prophet of the system's inevitable demise. The book will make a serious attempt to understand the way the system works.

What the Book Does

The book is in two parts: the first Part examines the nature and origins of the crisis, draws some conclusions and ends with a chapter treating of some false assumptions in much current government thinking about its causes and possible remedies; the second part makes proposals for what could be done, at the national and international level, in the long term, the medium term and immediately.

Part I *How It Is*

In the first Part, the book starts by looking at what is called the financial crisis, in Asia and in Russia and spreading outward by contagion as money loses its value. It asks what is money and how it affects the real world we live in, where money means having enough for a drink or two when we have paid for our food and lodgings and how much we can borrow or get on credit and how we shall pay off our debts and the interest charges.

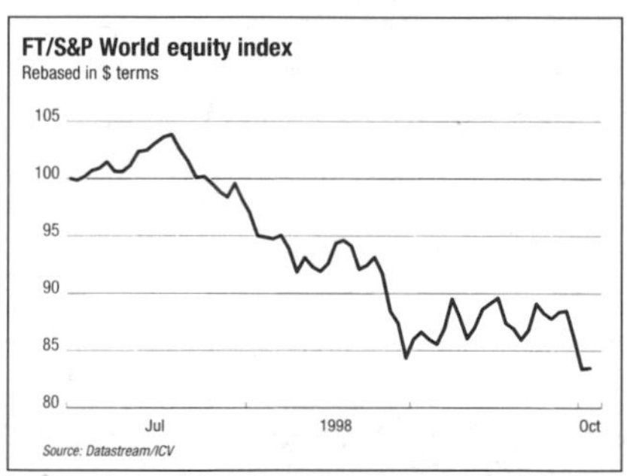

When we run up an overdraft, the bank seems to be quite concerned, and the manager writes tough letters asking how we intend to pay up; but what the papers are saying is that the banks lent billions in Asia and Russia on dubious prospectuses and look like losing a lot of it; and it appears that they have often done this before. In the 1930s the whole pack of cards collapsed and millions all over the world were unemployed and this could happen again. How can this be?

To answer this question, the book goes back a bit in time to ask about markets. What function do they perform apart from being places where we go shopping? Why have governments been saying that these things are best left to the "market". What is it? And why are governments now having to rescue the banks but do nothing about the Courtaulds or Rover lay-offs?

What, then, is this capitalist system, what drives it and why does it seem to generate inequalities and instability? And where do all these mergers lead – of giant companies like Exxon and Mobil or Daimler and Chrysler forming themselves into mega-corporations?

Globalisation is said to be the explanation for everything. But wasn't the

British Empire almost global? Is it just that the Brits aren't top dogs any more? United States military forces and the United States dollar now rule the world. But are the Americans doing any better? There was a collapse of share prices in New York in October 1998, and everyone seems to fear a Wall Street crash like 1929. Has nobody learn't any lessons? Or is it that money can now whizz electronically around the world so much faster, when speculation becomes the name of the game and all the rules of the game are relaxed? Is it beyond control? Is there nothing governments can do?

For thirty years after the Second World War, up to the 1970s, it seemed to be possible to exercise some control. Standards of living rose everywhere. Nearly everyone had a job, at least in Europe, and the poor countries which had been European colonies began to catch up. For the last 25 years, all that has changed. Unemployment has become endemic. While the rich have become richer, the poor have become poorer, not only in the poor countries but in the rich countries too. How could this have come about? It seems that there have been

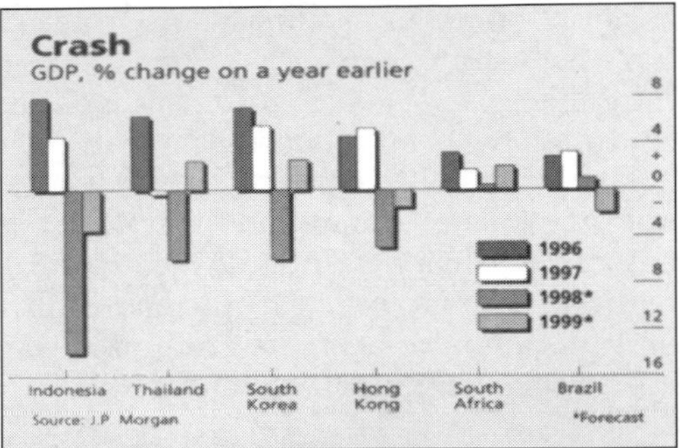

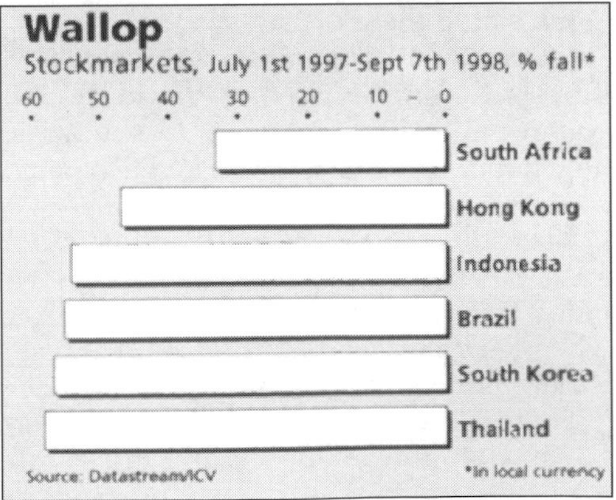

cycles of boom and slump before, some short ones and some long ones, but what causes them?

In these 25 years government policies have changed. Government controls have been reduced. The value of money has been given priority and the value of labour has been degraded. What has followed has been not only unemployment and inequality, but also much slower growth in output and living standards generally. Taxes on the rich have been reduced. Labour organisation has been circumscribed. Flexibility and deregulation have been the order of the day. None of this has worked and the whole environment has suffered.

Part II *What Could Be Done About It*

Keynesian measures maintained full employment and some degree of equality for thirty years after the Second World War. How did they work and why were they abandoned? They were said to cause prices to rise. What is price inflation and is it a danger to all? Businesses are asking for lower interest rates and some governments support this request. Will that create jobs? Governments already spend a large part of national incomes. Should they spend more to create jobs? Can taxing the rich help the poor and also those on middle incomes? What is the best way to develop a true social concern in politics?

Globalisation perhaps means that Keynesian measures won't work in a single country. Would common action by European governments work, even world-wide cooperation in recovery? Some people are pressing instead for national protection against foreign supplies, especially from poor countries. But does not that further enfeeble them as markets, already weakened as they are by their foreign debts? The international bankers say that the poor must pay up, but they can't if we won't buy from them. Could we not get the bankers to work according to more sensible rules? What would these be?

International cooperation was what the victorious Allies decided on after they had won the Second World War. But capitalism is a competitive system which does not seem to lend itself to cooperation. Moreover, the new technology leads to less and less demand for labour, and to every one competing, individuals and countries, for what work is going. Would it be possible to agree on shorter working time everywhere instead of overwork for some and no work for others? The economy of the future is seen by many information technology experts as becoming a network economy, which may not need all the giant companies and financial intermediaries we have today. Would that still need the private ownership of capital?

There is much talk today of a "third way" between the state plan as the Soviet Union developed it and the so-called "free" market of capitalism.

The idea is of a humanised capitalism. Is that possible? And what about the alternative of a humanised socialism? What would that mean in terms of democratic planning using the new information technology? Today, there are many people, especially young people, who feel that they want to live very personal and individual lives. What alternative forms of social ownership would interest them to ensure cooperative and coordinated endeavour?

Such medium-term and long-term alternatives can perhaps help us to avoid future crises and catastrophes, but they do not get us out of the current mess. What could be done to help the Asians, the Russians, the Africans and Latin Americans, whose troubles are spreading the world over? If more of the same free market medicine doesn't work when combined with the rescue packages, what should governments be expected to do to create jobs ? Is there new hope in the determination of the new political leaders in Europe to put full employment at the top of their agenda. What would this mean in detail and how would it all be paid for? It is a global crisis, and action could not be limited to Europe. Nor can it all be done by decisions coming from above.

In conclusion, what is most needed is a change of ideas. Is it possible to bring together an alliance of all those who have begun to think in new ways about wealth and poverty, about work and leisure, about gender relations, about health and education for all, about fair trade, about the dignity of the aged and the disabled, about cooperation in place of competition? If this were possible it would be a powerful new force in world affairs. This book says, 'yes it is', and tries to show how to do it.

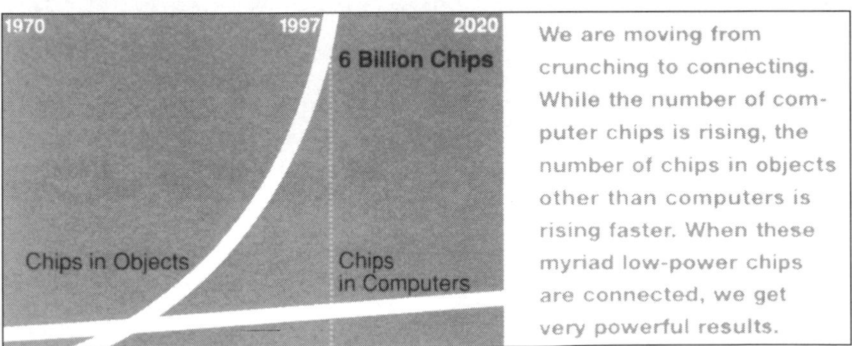

We are moving from crunching to connecting. While the number of computer chips is rising, the number of chips in objects other than computers is rising faster. When these myriad low-power chips are connected, we get very powerful results.

Part One

How It Is

CHAPTER 1

What Crisis?

There is lot of talk about a world crisis. What is it?

We think of a crisis as a time of great difficulty and danger, but a turning point also, when things might get better or worse according to what action we take. The Chinese are more optimistic: the character they use for our word 'crisis' combines the idea of opportunity with that of danger. Many people are aware of a crisis in their lives today. This is generally an economic crisis – of jobs, mortgages, pensions. And behind this there is a political crisis about how the economic crisis might be solved – by national government, by combined action in Europe or world-wide.

But what we are hearing about now is a financial crisis. Billions of £s are reported today, as this is written (October 2nd., 1998), to have been knocked off the value of shares on the Stock Exchange in London. Mr Gordon Brown, Britain's Chancellor of the Exchequer, has flown to Washington for an emergency meeting of the Finance Ministers of the richest countries. A top American financial analyst claims that the situation is more dangerous than it has been for 50 years. What does it all mean for us and our jobs? See what happened to Graham Jones in Durham (Box 1).

What is Money?

The baht is the name of the currency in Thailand, like the £ sterling here.

What do we want money for? Well, obviously we use it as a means of exchange, to buy things with and we use it as a unit of value for measuring. But it is also used as a store of value, in a bank account or in a savings account or in some form of capital – holdings of government stocks or shares in a company. Nearly all business is done on credit, that is the power to obtain goods or work done before payment, on the trust that payment will be made. The more money you have the easier it is to get credit, and the less interest you will have to pay for it.

If you have no store of money, you will have to pay up front for what you want, or borrow, and that will mean paying interest to the lender. He – and it generally is he – will charge interest according to the risk which he thinks is involved and the length of time that credit is needed for. Banks will want to know what regular income you have or assets you own before deciding to lend. Assets might be your house or other property, which you may have to mortgage – meaning hand over the ownership until the debt is paid. The interest rate on your credit card is very high because your only asset is your salary cheque.

Box 1. Chill East Wind at Your Doorstep

'When the Thai baht was devalued, Graham Jones didn't notice much nor care. Now 15 months later, he is on the dole, has little hope of a new job and is all too aware of the world downturn. RORY CARROLL shows how the Asian crisis spread through the global economy to claim the job of a barman in Whitley Bay.'

Fifteen months after the baht was devalued Graham checked out the new adverts in the Jobcentre on Whitley Road for the third time that day, ignoring the gawking bus passengers outside.

Apart from the scratching of phone numbers on to notepads the centre was silent. There were plenty of telesales jobs but Graham wasn't sure if he could endure the tedium. All he had done since leaving school was work in bars and restaurants and he enjoyed it. Except when it was dead.

"You can only clean a table so many times. Upstairs was busy but downstairs me and the barman had nothing to do. People just weren't going out."

He wasn't surprised when he was fired. "One pint served all night. It couldn't go on. It's just the way businesses go." Graham zipped up his jacket and walked home.

The ripples from Bangkok turned into a wave and washed away his job. There are thousands like him in Britain, maybe tens of thousands. No one knows how many.

The contagion is multiplying and feeding into the economy, affecting millions of people in tiny different ways. Economists say the chain reaction cauld end in a full-scale global depression not seen since the 1930s.

Time will tell whether the ripples from Bangkok dousing Whitley Bay become tidal waves sweeping jobs from the western world, including yours.

Story in *The Guardian*, G2, 28.10.98

There is a vast structure of credit in any economy at any time, like a pack of cards built up into a pyramid, all based on the assumption that payment will in the end be made and that the assets that form the bottom layer of the pack retain the money value that they were originally estimated at. Pull the bottom out and what happens? To change the metaphor from cards to mechanics, all the different layers of borrowing based on the basic assets are referred to as gearing or leverage, i.e. the ratio of fixed interest debt on top of the base of equity or ownership rights.

There are many different kinds of money, not only national currencies like the Thai baht and £ sterling, but money for different purposes – coins, notes and cheques and bills of exchange, which are an IOU, a form of credit that can be used for making payments. A very important form of credit consists of the bonds offered by governments and big companies for their borrowings. These are in effect promises to pay at a fixed rate of interest over a certain period of time. They are needed because of the time it takes for governments to collect in taxes and other payments and for companies to realise in final sales the goods or services that they were producing.

One of the aspects of the current financial crisis was the collapse of the bond market. Those who had been lending money prefer liquidity, that is cash and money on call. Those who had been borrowing wind down their debts. The result is that all business slows down. It is a mad system: when things are going well, money is pumped into the economy, exaggerating the boom; then when things turn bad, the money pours out again making the subsequent slump even worse. Here is what a leading American economist has to say about the Asian crisis:

17th Century money dealers. *Digital technology today.*

Box 2. Boom and Slump

'In 1996 alone foreign banks lent the countries now in crisis more than $100 billion and non-bank investors poured in tens of billions more. These enormous inflows allowed Asian countries to spend far more than their incomes. In the second half of 1997, however, those same banks called in more than $50 billion in loans .'

'And what was demanded as a condition for emergency IMF support? ... Instead of trying to prevent or even alleviate the looming slumps in their economies, they were told to follow policies which would actually deepen those slumps.'

Paul Krugman, 'A Crisis of Confidence', *New Republic* , Washington, September, 1998

Money and the Real Economy

The IMF is the International Monetary Fund that is supposed to help countries in financial difficulty, but the policies it recommends are always concerned with cutting government spending, often spending on the poor and the unemployed; and that, as Mr Krugman says, only results in making things worse.

So the crisis is not just about money. There is obviously a more general economic crisis. Factories are closing down in Britain, including some of the most advanced in the country, with the loss of thousands of jobs. This is happening not only in the UK but throughout Europe. Already before the Asian crisis broke, unemployment was high. In France, Germany, Italy, Spain and Belgium unemployment was hitting over 10% of the workforce and if we counted all the 'economically inactive' who would like to be active in the UK the figure would be similar here. Now, the economies of Japan and East Asia and Russia are all in actual decline, a decline that has been accelerating in the last months. Asian countries are flogging their micro-chips at $1.50 in place of $10 a unit. Countries like Russia which produce oil and other minerals and agricultural raw materials are facing sharply declining prices.

Britain's Chancellor Gordon Brown tells us that he thinks the drop in economic activity in the UK will only be on a small scale and short-lived, but others are more doubtful. **At least a third of the world economy is in the grip of a recession that could easily deepen into a world slump of the same proportions as that of the 1930s.** International trade, which has been growing faster than national output for some years, is expected to grow this year at only about 5% instead of earlier figures of around 10%. The prices of company shares on the stock markets of the world are well below the high levels of a few months ago and have been subject to falls of as much on average as 5% in one day. There are widespread jitters about the possibility of a real slump developing. Is it just a 'crisis of confidence', which we should not talk about in case we undermine confidence still further?

Wall Street, 1929.

The slump of the 1930s left nearly three million unemployed in the UK, which was then over 20% of the workforce. There were over 15 million unemployed in the United States in 1933, 25% of the work force. It began with the collapse of a group of banks in Central Europe leading to the crash of share prices on the US stock exchange on Wall Street in New York, amounting to a 90% fall. It only really ended with rearmament spending at the close of the decade. But it wasn't just a financial crisis. In the real economy, wages had for some years been falling behind profits as output was increased year by year. People couldn't buy all the goods that were being produced. The same has been happening in the last decade.

The present crisis started with the collapse of a number of financial institutions in Japan and East Asia, and was followed by financial collapse in Russia. There is talk of contagion: where next? One of the largest United States financial institutions, Long Term Capital Management (LTCM), a major hedge fund (a kind of insurance against changing prices) has had to be rescued by other banks, lest worse befall. Once again, the fear is that falling money will help to bring down still further the real economy of production of goods and services. In the mean time, cronies must be rescued, but what is the link between a financial crisis and the real economy?

Unemployed marchers, 1930s.

Box 3. 'Crony Capitalism'

'...there was at least an appearance of crony capitalism' at LTCM, where 'one of the principals was a former vice chairman of the FED [the central bank of the USA], which led the rescue effort.' While South Korea, Thailand and Indonesia were heavily criticised for acquiring mountains of debt, the 'magnitude of the debt at (LTCM) was unbelievable ... somewhere between one to one and a half trillion [thousand billion] dollars, based on a capital of between three to five billion dollars... And American and Swiss banks were lending to this highly leveraged hedge fund.'

Joseph Stiglitz, World Bank chief economist, speaking at the Annual Board Meeting of the UN Conference on Trade and Development, 19.10.1998

What Happened in Russia

What happened in Russia in 1998 is instructive as to the link between money and the real economy. There was an economic and financial crisis in East Asia, which led to a sharp decline in the demand for oil; the oil price collapsed. Russia, which relied on oil exports, could not pay the interest on foreign borrowings. A $23 billion financial package from the IMF and Japan was supplied, but this failed to cover Russia's outstanding debts. Foreign investors lost confidence and pulled out and Russia's capitalists then also sold out. Russia's currency, the rouble, lost half its value.

Behind this, the past use of Russia's oil exports to pay for the luxury imports and the wealth transfers out of the country by the new elite left the government with no money to pay the civil servants, the soldiers or the coal miners. A huge gap opened up between the incomes of the rich elite and those of the mass of the people. For them, much of the economy now operates on a system of barter, the exchange of goods and services taking place without the use of money.

It is said in the West that Russia's problems stem from its inability to service foreign debt or maintain the value of the rouble. But that arose from internal problems leading to loss of foreign confidence. The West in the shape of the IMF had been insisting on opening up the economy to free trade and financial liberalisation before it was ready for it. We can take it from the words of the British economist, Lord Desai:

Box 4. Mistaken Liberalisation

'Russia was rushed headlong into liberalisation by economists who had no knowledge of the country's history or institutions. They hurriedly began fitting Russia into their macroeconomic models ...'

Meghnad Desai, 'Russia Must Put Bread Before Theory?', Guardian, 21.09.98

Having abandoned Soviet controls over the economy, Russia simply did not have any systems to prevent massive theft and fraud by its new robber capitalists, home grown and foreign, let alone for getting them to pay their taxes.

Devaluations of currencies have followed elsewhere, in other countries where commodity prices have fallen and reckless, speculative investment has been rife – not only in Asia but in Latin America – and these might go further. China and Hong Kong might follow. Fears are growing that a number of large Japanese financial institutions could fail and that the prices of some big Japanese company shares could fall to a level where a general melt down would occur. Then large numbers of companies would be bankrupt and their workers made unemployed.

For years we have been told by bankers and finance ministers that what the world economy needs is stability. That was interpreted to mean putting stable prices and a stable money ahead of full employment as the aim of government policy. And what seemed only to be the policy of Conservative governments in Britain has been adopted by New Labour. So we have had fairly stable prices and we have lost full employment, and the net result today is total financial instability.

The bankers who were supposed to be the guardians of our savings and the guarantors of stability have been shown up as the source of the turbulence. The attacks of the speculators have been self-fulfilling and the banks have done nothing to control them. Indeed, they have encouraged them by asking for ever more financial liberalisation. Look at what the most respectable authorities are saying about them.

Box 5. The Banks and Financial Contagion

'Much of banking history consists of one speculative bubble after another, from Dutch bulbs in the 17th. century to property in the 1980s – and now emerging markets and hedge funds in the 1990s. Each tends to be fuelled by an explosion of credit, a wave of unwarranted optimism and a subsequent mispricing of risk.'

Editorial, 'Handle with Care', *The Economist*, October 3rd., 1998

'Since the onset of the Asian crisis 15 months ago, financial contagion has spread insidiously, and now routinely, to the point where markets are being destabilised on a global basis. The spill-over effects, initially from Asia and now from Russia, have hurt countries regardless of the soundness of their economic policies.'

John Plender, *Financial Times*, 21.09.98

'I do think we have to bring the existing instabilities to a level of stability reasonably shortly, to prevent the contagion from really spilling over and creating some very significant further difficulties for all of us.'

Alan Greenspan, Chairman of the US Federal Reserve Bank, 23.09.98

' A paper from the World Bank has managed to identify banking crises in as many as 69 countries since the late 1970s ... often conjoined with currency crises, of which there have been 87 since 1975 according to a paper co-authored by Joseph Stiglitz, chief economist of the World Bank... An IMF paper estimates that, almost incredibly, three quarters of IMF member countries experienced 'significant bank sector problems between 1980 and 1985''

Martin Wolf, 'Frail Orthodoxy', *Financial Times*, 21.10.98

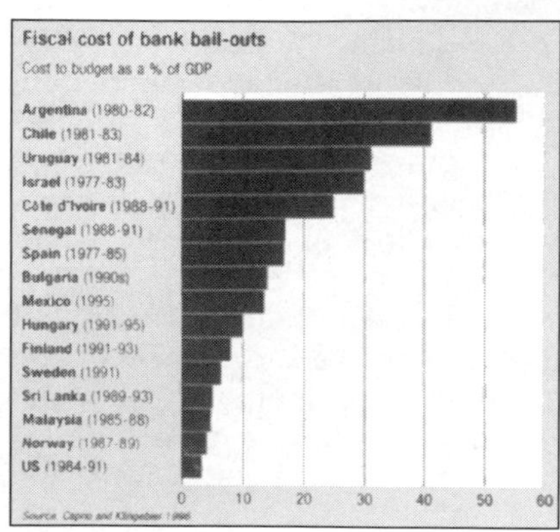

According to a Table in Martin Wolf's article, governments in 16 different countries in the last decade have been bailing out their banks, at a cost on average of 20% of their national income. How can it be that banks get into such trouble, and in a period when the preservation of money values had been given priority by governments? And why is the latest banking crisis so much more serious than the previous ones?

CHAPTER 2

How We Came To Be Where We Are

What then is the connection between this money economy with all its speculations and uncertainties and the real economy in which we live and work? What went wrong first?

The Origin of Markets

To answer this question, we have to go back a little in history. Once upon a time nearly all families lived in the country and built their own houses, grew their own food and made their own clothes and coverings. Then some people began to live in towns and to work in workshops and offices, but most families stayed on working on the land. That is how it still is for at least half the world's people who live in poor countries, often called

Amsterdam market in the 17th Century.

'Third World' countries, which were once colonies of the European empires like the British Empire.

In the towns that grew up everywhere, regular markets were held just as they are today, at which goods from the country and from the towns were exchanged, first through barter and then using money. Merchants began to bring goods to these markets from far away places, things like salt and pepper for seasoning and precious metals for money.

Most prices were set in these markets by bargaining according to what seemed a fair exchange, but the goods coming from far away had a special value as the result of their scarcity as well as the cost of their transport. There was generally plenty of competition in the market, except in times of famine, so that nobody could get away with an unfair price, but the merchants who brought goods from a distance often had no competition, and therefore a virtual monopoly, and could push the price up.

Today we probably do most of our shopping not in the markets but in the super markets. There the goods on the shelves may come from every part of the world – shoes from China, dresses from Hong Kong, jeans from the United States, fruit from Spain and Israel, vegetables from Africa and Latin America, chocolate from cocoa beans grown in Ghana, coffee from Brazil, tea from India; and if we buy a TV set, a car or a computer it probably comes from Japan or from Korea. There is still plenty of competition among the producers and the retailers, although there are suppliers who now operate in between the producers and the shops with something near a monopoly.

These are the giant international companies like Nestlé and Philip Morris who draw their supplies from many producers and advertise their brands everywhere. Among many other products, these two control between them, for example, 71% of the UK coffee market and can pretty well fix the price. With companies like these, there is not much place for bargaining in the market now, but we can of course refuse to buy things that we think are not good value for money and, if enough of us do that, the supplier will have to make changes or go out of business.

Wage Earners, Employers and Markets

At different times in history in different countries, the people have been dispossessed of their land holdings by clearances, evictions and enclosures, and other violent means. Then they have had to go to find work for an employer, perhaps in the country, more often in the towns and cities as these grew up. They came to depend on an employer with the necessary capital for machines and tools for them to work with. They would then be paid a wage for their work. There might be plenty of different employers to go to, but there were occasions when none of them wanted to take on workers. Wages were then driven very low and men and women found themselves unemployed.

There was a market for labour because it became like any other commodity something to be bought and sold. But in this market the buyers and sellers had very unequal power. Those who had money enough to form capital could use it to make more money, as merchants by buying commodities cheap and selling them dear, or as industrialists by buying labour cheap and selling the products of labour for more than they paid for the labour. **This fundamental inequality between capital and labour, whether in relation to commodity producers in the colonies or to industrial workers at home, lies at the heart of the whole explanation we shall find for the current world crisis.**

All capitalists have to make profits in this way, not just to reinvest in their business, but to keep up with the going rate of profit everywhere. If they don't, they will be unable to survive in a competitive market. They may go bust or get taken over or simply fail to get credit for future activities. Capital is only worth what profit can be made from it, but this is to argue in a circle, because the rate of profit in turn depends in part on the value of capital and when this has been invested in obsolete machinery it loses its value.

A bankruptcy soon reveals the market value of the capital of a business; it is worth only what the buildings, plant and machinery can be sold off for by a liquidator anxious to rescue as much as possible as quickly as possible for the creditors. New businesses can then be started up with such assets bought at knock-down prices.

Box 6. Capital Devaluation and Crisis

'Devaluations in this sense will occur when developments in the macro-economy make it *temporarily* impossible for individual capitals to continue operations because of low and even negative rates of profit. A general economic crisis is then necessary to restore the economic conditions in which it is once more possible for individual capitals to resume the accumulation process.'

Robin Murray, *Upper Clyde Shipyards: The Anatomy of Bankruptcy*, p.30, Spokesman Books, 1972

The macro-economy is the world of governments' and state spending and of international trade. So it seems that a general economic crisis is actually necessary for capital accumulation to continue. Profits are used for capital accumulation in larger and larger amounts. But this means that labour receives a smaller share of the value produced, not necessarily a lower wage but a smaller share, and some might be unemployed. Then a point must come when wage and salary earners and the unemployed cannot buy back all the extra goods and services that can be produced with capital invested in more up to date equipment. **Such growing**

Upper Clyde shipyard workers, 1970s.

inequalities following upon a period of rapid capital accumulation are the first and last cause of all crises.

To ameliorate the crisis, governments can take action to redistribute incomes to some degree from the rich to the poor, and this is what they have done in the past. Although it can only be effective to a limited extent because the problem keeps recurring, governments have been forced to take such action by the pressure of popular opinion. To defend themselves and their families, men and women have for long banded together in unions. These have not only bargained with employers on behalf of their members, but they have specifically demanded from the government of their country the right to work or to some protection when they were out of work.

As a result, governments have become responsible for more and more rules and regulations to protect people from distress and disorder inside the country as well as from threats and attacks from outside and to provide for education and health and social services. These public services then had to be paid for by taxes designed to take rather more proportionately from the rich – persons and companies – than from the poor, and so to some extent redistribute incomes.

In some countries governments went further and began to manage production themselves and to fix prices and wages. They all did this in wartime; and in some countries with Communist governments like the Soviet Union and even with Socialist governments as in the UK such wartime measures were continued after the war. But generally, production and distribution of goods and services were left to private businesses. It was thought that competition in the market between different companies seeking a profitable return on their capital was the best way of allocating resources to meet people's needs. This opinion received confirmation with the collapse of the Soviet planned economy.

Prices and wages are then settled in most economies by what is still called 'the market'. This covers all the different markets – for capital the Stock Exchanges, for other forms of money the money market and foreign exchange market, for raw materials the several commodity markets, for land and houses the property market, for labour the Labour Exchange or Job Centre, as we now know it, and for goods and services, not so much the old market places as the new supermarkets. But the labour market, as we have seen, and the commodity markets too, while they appear to be based upon some sort of equal exchange, in fact serve to conceal fundamental inequalities.

The Big Companies Rule – OK?

In our regular economic dealings, most of us no longer bargain in a market place, but bargaining goes on all the time among the people with money – in the stock markets, money markets and commodity markets. Our trade union may bargain for us over our wages, but, while we can 'shop around'

for 'bargains', mainly we have to take it or leave it in making our purchases, and even in finding a job. In fact there is much less competition between suppliers than may appear. The shops and supermarkets may be in competition, but they may all have a quite limited number of suppliers of any particular product.

As we saw in the case of coffee, two or three very big companies operating world-wide control the supplies of most commodities. This is true of coffee, cocoa, sugar or tobacco and most of the bread grains and minerals. The seven giant petrol companies can manage the market and settle the price at the pumps between them.

Box 7. Mega-Corporations

'...some multinational corporations command more wealth and economic power than most states do. Indeed, of the world's 100 largest economies 50 are megacorporations. The 350 largest corporations now account for 40% of global trade, and their turnover exceeds the GDP of many countries. .. General Motors more than Turkey or Denmark ... Ford more than South Africa ...Toyota, Exxon and Shell each more than Norway or Poland ...IBM more than Pakistan or Malaysia ... Unilever, Nestlé and Sony each more than Egypt or Nigeria...the top five corporations double the GDP of all South Asia.'

UN Development Programme, *Human Development Report, 1997*, New York , 1997, p.92

NOTE: GDP is net of imports; Turnover is *not* net of inputs. So, turnover is somewhat exaggerated.

Much of the half of the world's trade that is now carried on by a few hundred giant companies takes place as inter-national exchanges inside the companies themselves, since they have branches and subsidiaries all over the world. So most prices are fixed in transfer pricing between the branches of big companies, often with the aim of tax avoidance, by making the profit appear to be made in a country with low taxes. It is alleged that Mr Murdoch's companies pay no taxes in the United Kingdom.

In recent years it has been thought by most governments that they should interfere as little as possible in 'the market'. This really means governments leaving it to the big companies to move their capital where they wish. The big companies are generally associated with one or more big banks which put together the financial packages for their investments and advise on where their capital will be most profitably employed. This is assumed to mean the same as where peoples' needs are being met. But the pull of the market is the pull of money; rich people's needs, or at least their demands, will have the most pull. And, as we have seen, some of the investment may be highly speculative

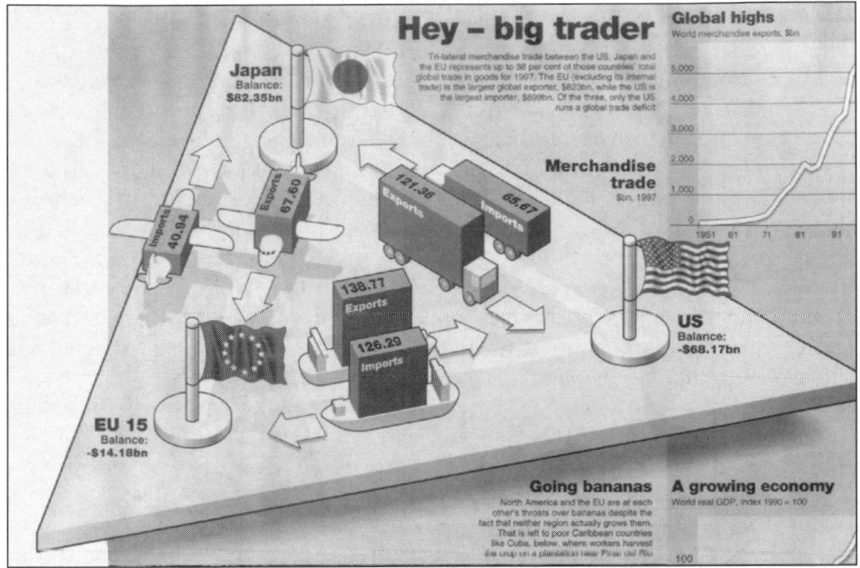

Governments can tax the rich, both individuals and companies, but they are afraid to go too far lest they drive them away to invest elsewhere or to hide their money in offshore tax havens, and the governments lose what taxes they have been getting. To prevent a general loss of confidence in the system, governments will generally bail out banks which get into real trouble, and this may involve them in very large expenditures, as we saw earlier.

What governments have come to fear most is a fall in the value of their country's currency as the result of price inflation. This means that those who have money all round the world lose confidence in holding this currency and investing in the country. So governments have come to concentrate mainly on ensuring that prices don't rise too much and certainly want to avoid an accelerating rate of inflation, which rapidly reduces the value of the money concerned.

Because governments today think that the main cause of inflation is pressure for higher wages, they argue that it is a good thing to have some unemployment, so that wage earners dare not push too hard for higher wages. Governments therefore seek to hold down any spending and particularly public spending which would generate full employment. There are of course many other reasons for inflation – higher cost of imports such as when oil prices were hiked, collapse of the currency as in Russia today and general shortages of goods as in wartime; but also when firms are operating below their full capacity they have to charge more and a large company with little competition can really fix the price.

Governments and Capital Movements

This is where the money economy comes in as the source of trouble in the real economy. The capitalist economic system is driven by the return to capital. Nothing else really matters except that owners and controllers of capital obtain the going rate of profit from their investment. If they do not achieve this, they will be forced out of business. The value of their capital depends on continuing profits, but this at any time includes the expectation of future profits. This is what determines prices on the Stock Exchanges and the expectations may be looking several years ahead. A great deal of speculation is then added to those expectations. But all the calculations depend on the value of the money when it is spent and the expectation that it will hopefully return one day with a margin of profit.

The value of money – in different currencies and in different investments – is constantly changing. So, we have beautiful new factories for making electronics in Scotland or Wales or Durham built with government aid, and then being found to be worthless and closed down or never opened up – partly because new technology has overtaken them, partly because demand has everywhere declined, and partly because the relative values of the £ sterling and the Thai *baht* or Korean *won* have changed. Sterling has become more expensive and the *baht* and *won* cheaper. So production is moved back to Thailand or Korea.

If governments want to influence such decisions they have either to offer financial aid to the transnational companies, which shift their investments from place to place, that is with a subsidy to be paid for by the general tax payer, or they have to take action to change their currency values. British manufacturers who export much of their output have been complaining bitterly at the expensive £ in foreign exchange markets. The government can influence the world-wide value of its currency chiefly by raising or lowering interest rates to attract or repel flows of funds. But there are problems about doing this.

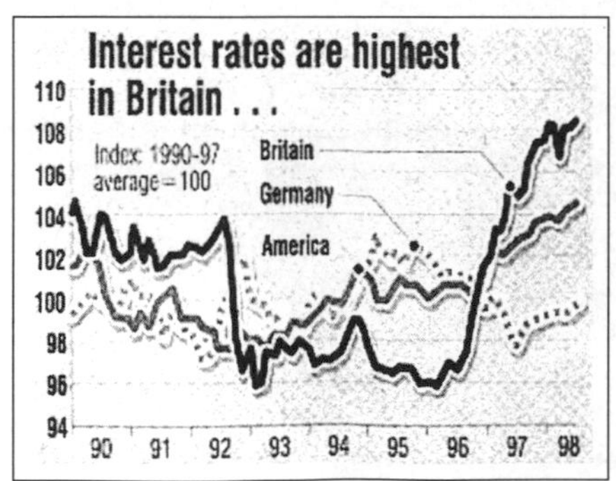

Different National Interest Rates

Interest rates vary greatly from country to country for reasons that are difficult for governments to alter. Those rich people and companies with money to move round the world will leave it in countries where they believe that it is safe and particularly safe from the value of that country's currency falling. A poor country like Ghana selling commodities with uncertain prices will have to offer very high rates to persuade anyone to hold their money in *cedis*. A rich country like Switzerland selling machine tools and tourism need offer only a low rate for holdings of Swiss francs. Above all the United States, which is the supplier of the dollar, used by all countries as the international reserve currency, can borrow cheaply from the rest of the world for its own consumption and for investing to gain higher rates than it pays for borrowing. It is within very narrow limits, therefore, that any other government than the US can influence the interest rates in its country since the world money market is an open one, and governments have been under strong pressure, as we have seen, to keep it that way.

How then do interest rates affect the general state of any economy? The way it works is complicated and is best set out schematically:

Box 8. How Interest Rates Work

High interest rates
- are used to deflate the economy, i.e. check growth especially of wage demands and to check inflation
- and attract foreign funds
- and result in high currency values which make imports cheaper but exports more expensive
- and encourage big firms to invest abroad with the strong currency, instead of at home in a deflated market.

Low interest rates
- are used to encourage growth and investment at home, but they
- tend to create inflation
- repel foreign funds
- and result in low currency values which make imports more expensive but exports cheaper
- discourage firms from investing abroad and encourage home investment

---

Governments have to balance the advantages and disadvantages at any time of having high or low interest rates, and often give the job to a Central Bank or Monetary Committee, as in the UK, with a general remit – in the UK it is to keep down inflation, and not to maintain employment at a high level.

There is at present much argument about this remit, which is said to be the best way to get economic growth. Many would disagree, but governments have at all times to consider the effects of their actions on business decisions, including the bankers' exposure, as well as on the well-being of their peoples; and all this within a global environment of money for ever on the move from one location, investment or currency, to another.

It is not surprising if this inevitably creates serious tensions, especially when the global activities of businessmen and bankers are deliberately concealed from public view. The fact that their decisions and the reasons for their decisions are not transparent makes possible all the speculation that goes on in the money markets. If everything was known there would be nothing to speculate about. There is no market in magnesium, because unlike almost all other minerals there are practically unlimited quantities to be extracted from sea water. No one can 'corner' the supply.

The power of a Central Bank is a major issue in the establishment of an Economic and Monetary Union (EMU) in Europe to which all but the UK, Denmark and Sweden of the present members of the European Union (what in Britain we just call 'Europe' or the 'Common Market') are agreed upon. The British Government is waiting for a referendum to decide the question, to be held at the time of or after the next General Election. The main objection in Britain is that the crucial financial decisions, and particularly the setting of interest rates, would be taken entirely out of the Government's hands and placed in those of a European Central Bank, which will have the same remit – to keep down inflation – as the Bank of England, but if not changed, may be expected to exercise this more strictly and with even less concern for employment.

The fact is that most governments have even now very limited power to set their own interest rates – too low and people with money will take their money away, too high and businesses in their country, and the government too, which rely on borrowing, will have to cut back. When some people complain that British sovereignty is being lost to some faceless bankers in Europe, one answer is that this sovereignty only ever lasted for the brief period between the German Central Bank changing its interest rate and the Bank of England having to follow suit.

CHAPTER 3

A World Economy

What all this means is that individual governments, even of very big countries, can't act on their own, but have to watch what other countries are doing and in particular what the big companies and banks are doing. Other countries may be producing goods more cheaply, with cheaper labour or less regulation and lower taxes; the big companies may prefer, therefore, to switch their capital for investment there. Big companies want to be able not only to move their goods around freely – called 'free trade' – but also, as we have seen, to move their capital around freely – called 'financial liberalisation'. **Most of the hundred or so very big companies like Ford Motors or Unilever or Cadbury Schweppes which dominate their markets produce more now outside their country of origin than they do inside.**

Governments and Globalisation

Capital has always been invested on a global scale. What is new is the increased size of the big companies and their capacity to switch production

from one place to another. This is why governments have to fit in with these international companies' needs and demands, if they want the companies' investment to come their way. It is not, as some people suggest, that governments have lost their power to act. They still have the powers, but they have to use them with an eye to the big companies. If they want Mr Murdoch's money, and the support of the newspapers that he owns, to take an example, they must let him buy Manchester United.

Governments not only have to keep an eye on the big companies and the banks, they have also to watch what is happening in the markets. This means not only the sales of goods and services to other countries and the purchases from them and the balance between the two, but the total movements of money in and out of the country. Most of us only want foreign currency for a holiday abroad and this can be balanced with foreigners' need for £s when visiting Britain. Compared with the huge sums moving in payments for imports and exports, and especially by the big companies' buying and selling and the banks' financial operations, the tourists' payments are quite small.

Every day in the markets for foreign exchange, there is a balance between the amounts of any one currency, like the £ sterling, being bought and being sold. If people want to buy more £s than are being changed into other currencies, then the value of the £ will go up. If people want to sell more, then it will go down. The value will also be affected by expectations of what will happen in the future, and this will include expectations about the rate of interest you get if you hold your money in £s compared with rates elsewhere and about the general economic situation of any country, whose currency you hold.

The value of the Russian rouble has collapsed, although the Russian government raised interest rates and spent its own reserves of foreign currency to stem the fall, chiefly because people both in Russia and outside ceased to believe in the capacity of the Russian economy to recover and be able to pay its debts. But this is a vicious circle: money flows out because the economy is weak and that makes more money flow out. The only answer is to stem the flow and let the debts be paid later when the economy has recovered.

Box 9. Food or Theory in Russia

...the best thing that can happen to Russia is everything the IMF and the G7 [richest nations] do not want. It would also be the best thing for the world economy. This would be to grant Russia a holiday from liberalisation until it gets its domestic economy reconstructed. Like Japan or China, it could be allowed to concentrate on its own backyard for a while. When this is completed Russia can gradually re-enter the world economy.

Meghnad Desai, 'Russia Must Put Bread Before Theory', *Guardian*, 21.09.98

Unequal Starting Points

Any country can run into debt for any number of reasons – the results of wartime expenditure, a bad harvest, a rise in imported oil prices, a fall in its own commodity export prices, a big new investment programme. The International Financial Institutions, the International Monetary Fund (IMF) and the World Bank, were designed after the Second World War to help countries in such difficulties – the IMF with short term finance and financial regulation and the World Bank with long term loans and technical advice.

Several of the world's poorest countries have run up huge debts for all the above reasons and have been given help, but always on strict conditions, often called 'structural adjustments' or 'reforms' – requiring that they open up their economies to free trade and financial liberalisation. They are still in trouble many years later, because the 'reforms' haven't worked. The reason is simple. They have different starting points.

The agriculture and industries of these countries simply couldn't compete, without some trade protection, in the world markets dominated by big companies; and when foreign exchange controls were lifted, the people in them who had money simply transferred their wealth to banks in Switzerland or to investments in real estate in Florida or Hawaii. This is what those with money in Russia have been doing. The latest proposal for opening up markets to the big companies' investment is the MAI (Multinational Agreement on Investment). This would restrict any government's right to interfere in world markets on behalf of its nationals.

Markets, however, only work well on certain conditions:

- **if the parties are roughly equal in bargaining power;**
- **if there is sufficient demand for the goods and services of all those who have something to offer, whether goods or services;**
- **where there is a real chance for newcomers to get in or protect themselves from others at higher levels of development;**
- **where there is some market regulation, protection against thieves and cheats and control over speculators;**
- **and where there is a political**

framework of law and order, social cohesion and infrastructure. Every country has some sort of regulation over its capital market and has a central bank which can act as a lender of last resort. There is no such regulator or banker on a world scale. The IMF and the World Bank were never given these powers. Although it was proposed at the time when they were established to do so, the United States government did not wish to see such powers in other hands than its own. The result is that increasing global liberalisation works in favour of the rich who can find money and markets more easily and survive bad times and to the disadvantage of the poor who cannot.

The result is cumulative: the rich become richer and the poor become poorer. And the advice which comes from the IMF and the World Bank is the same for all – to open up their markets to the goods and the capital of the world. But some markets and particularly the already rich markets are more attractive than the others. The poor markets simply become marginalised. As Africa has become poorer, flows of foreign investment there have dried up.

Box 10. Cheating the Poor

'We were told that if we had democracy, we would get funds. We had democracy, but no funds came. We were told if we had structural adjustments, foreign direct investment would come. We had Structural Adjustment Programmes, but no funds came. We were told if we had trade liberalisation and privatisation, investment would come, but none came. Now we are told we will get funds if there is a Multilateral Investment Agreement. You are trying to cheat Africa.'

Basoga Nsadhu, Finance Minister of Uganda, at a conference on MAI, staged by the World Trade Organisation in 1996

Capital Liberalisation and Financial Speculation

The money and foreign exchange markets are made all the more difficult for those who are relatively weak competitors, because they are the object of massive world-wide speculation. Vast sums of money are made (and lost) by speculating on the way prices are likely to move in the future. A young man working in the Singapore branch of Baring's bank lost millions in such operations and was jailed for it, but it became clear that the bank may have encouraged him, if not actually condoning the actions for which he was jailed. It is obvious that only those with such vast sums can gamble on such speculation. It is also obvious that, if large sums are tied up in speculative adventures, they are not available for investment in productive activity such as would create employment. The daily turnover of funds on the financial markets is today many hundred times that on the stock markets, where capital for business activity is raised.

The results of such speculation are that any country whose future economic development is thought to be in any way in doubt finds itself exposed to the most serious adverse pressure on the value of its currency. The story is well known of the huge profits made at the expense of the Bank of England by Mr George Soros, a financial speculator, in selling sterling in 1994, fully confident that it would have to be devalued when he could buy back at the lower price what he had sold at the higher price. Fortunes will equally have been made, as well as lost, out of the Russian rouble collapse.

Latin American countries seem likely to follow Russia down. Although these countries' economic relations with Russia are quite unimportant, and most large Latin American countries have relatively stable governments and have made structural adjustments in government finance, have raised interest rates and are pledged to continue with the liberalisation, privatisation and de-regulation of their economies, yet, because they have borrowed money on world markets, speculators have reduced their exposure in Latin America to make up for losses in Russia

It is not, however, only the weak players who suffer. The volatility of financial markets – huge up and down swings (and what we have seen is now called 'contagion' – weakness in one country or market spreading to others) are bad for everyone. Even Mr Soros has begun to complain. The fact is that the monetary theory employed to support financial liberalisation, which the big companies desired in order to be free to move their capital around, has been shown to be wanting .

The IMF was not given powers to regulate such capital flows. 50 years ago trade in goods and services was what mattered to the big companies; states were allowed to manage their capital. Now it is movements of capital that matter to them. It is not only that the IMF as an institution is secretive and arbitrary, (which the British Prime Minister, Tony Blair, complains of and wishes to reform), it operates increasingly on the principle of liberalisation, and the intention is to legalise this. Mr Blair, indeed, has indicated his support for extending liberalisation in the manner proposed by the OECD (the organisation of the advanced

industrialised countries) through the Multilateral Agreement on Investment (MAI).

There is, however, widespread public disquiet at the prospect of big companies being able to take the place of governments as the rulers of what we can do, not only economically but culturally. The protests were so strong in France at the freedom which would be allowed for TV programmes and films from the United States to flood the French media that Prime Minister Jospin has declared his government's resolute opposition to MAI. There have been movements of citizen protest in altogether 23 countries, amounting to what a Canadian writer has called the voice of 'global civil society'. But such liberalisation is not even economically sound.

Box 11. Failed Liberalisation

'The last 20 years have shown that complete liberalisation of capital flows is inefficient, due to volatility and contagion...Campaigns to rewrite the IMF articles to require full market liberalisation by all nations and OECD proposals to write full capital liberalisation into an MAI are without sound intellectual foundations and should be abandoned.'

John Eatwell (Lord Eatwell) and Lance Taylor 'International Capital Markets and the Future of Economic Policy' research project for the New School of Social Research, New York, September 1998

It is very much to be hoped that Mr Blair is listening. John Eatwell, a distinguished economist, was at one time a New Labour adviser. Mr Blair, prior to his proposals for reforming the IMF, wrote in the 'Internationalist' section of his Fabian pamphlet on *The Third Way* that 'We seek stronger international institutions for the management of trade, finance, the peaceful resolution of disputes, and to ensure swift response to pressing new problems, like the crises in Asia and Russia and the threat to the global environment.'

He instanced, however, the record of the European Union, NATO and the World Trade Organisation (WTO), and not of the United Nations (UN), which is the only truly world-wide international body. The first two are regional organisations and WTO, like MAI, is bitterly opposed by most of the Third World countries because its management policies have all worked in favour of the already industrialised countries. The management of trade and finance by international institutions has to reckon with the overwhelming power of the giant transnational companies and banks. These receive no mention in Mr Blair's picture of a 'modern dynamic economy'.

This 'new economy', he says, 'like the new politics – is radically different [from the past]. Services, knowledge, skills and small enterprises are its cornerstones. Most of its output cannot be weighed, touched or measured, its most valuable assets are knowledge and creativity.'

The mixture of metaphors is confusing. Cornerstones can be weighed, touched and measured. So can the output of small enterprises; and when it is measured it hardly begins to equate with the output of the giant transnational companies. Although more people may be employed in such small and medium sized enterprises, they have little power in the market and will generally be found to be sub-contractors or holders of franchises from the big manufacturing or retailing companies. It is the overwhelming power of these, generally transnationally operating, companies that is the central feature of the 'new economy', and it is they who are the main accumulators of the funds which have been whizzing round the world in recent years.

But the global economy is not just an economy of giant transnational companies. It is an economy dominated by United States capital, which seeks to bring the whole world within its control and which is now primarily a service economy not a manufacturing economy. This is the importance of MAI and increasing the power of the WTO or IMF over capital movements. The Russian crisis and the Asian crisis leave the United States in a position of even greater dominance and the US government will seek to keep it that way. First the Soviet Union and then Japan were serious rivals. They have neither of them been given the resources in their respective crises – a Marshall Plan for Russia or an Asia Fund for Japan – which would enable them to pose a serious challenge to American hegemony.

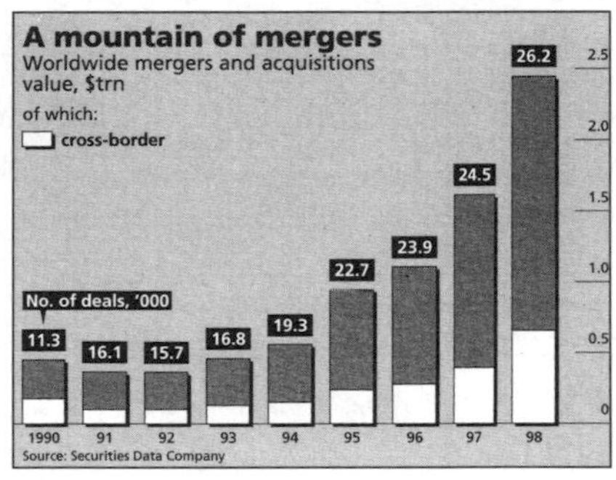

Europe and China remain the chief obstacles to a world of American capital, American billionaires, American banks, American insurance, American information technology, American TV and other media, and American retailing systems. The crisis is not just financial, nor even just economic. It is for the whole world a crisis of identity. But it is bound up with a crisis of American capitalism, in which the accumulation of capital in its American centre at the expense of the rest of the whole world begins to threaten the stability of the centre itself. Overcapitalisation – an equity market in the USA with stock values approaching 140% of national income, compared with 82% in the crash of 1929 – makes a stock market crash, according to many experts, entirely imaginable within a couple of years. And behind this lies the real economy in the USA, where profits have been rising for over a decade while wages have actually been falling – just as they did in the 1920s. That is the danger of globalism with a single centre.

CHAPTER 4

Origins of the Crisis

The troubles of today have not come upon us suddenly. They have been building up for a long time, and some of us have been giving warnings for some time. But no one listens to cries of 'Wolf! Wolf!', if the wolf doesn't appear at once. The papers are now full of criticism of the banks, stories of their greed and their incompetence, and of the danger of an American slump, but a few years or even months ago such stories were not listened to. It was said that all was for the best, the US economy continued to boom and current high unemployment levels in Europe would soon come down. The MEP, Ken Coates, with ex-MP Stuart Holland and myself, exchanged a whole series of letters in 1995 with Commissioners of the European Union (*Dear Commissioner*, published by Spokesman in 1996), warning them that their expectations of future growth rates were hopelessly optimistic. We were right, but how did we know?

Unemployed people protest in London, 1933.

For about thirty years after the Second World War, the world economy was progressing rather well, far better than in the pre-war years. Unemployment rates were low, more houses were built, new motorways and new schools and universities and hospitals. Governments followed the policies recommended by the economist, J.M. Keynes, of running a high level of government expenditure from increased taxation of the rich, to maintain full employment; policies which he believed would have avoided the 1930s slump. Not only did public spending grow, but private consumption grew with it. Cars and washing machines and TV sets and telephones became the possessions of more and more households.

Governments in Britain were not alone in pursuing Keynesian full employment policies and successfully expanding their peoples' incomes and expenditures. The Soviet Union and Japan joined the number of advanced industrial countries. China and even many of the poor countries, which had been European colonies, began to catch up as the result of the better prices they were getting for their commodities. Some especially in East Asia actually began to manufacture goods in their own industries, and to export these goods, even advanced electronics, to the rich countries' markets.

In the early 1970s this happy state of affairs began bit by bit to dissolve. The annual increases in productivity, that is output per person, on which the growth of living standards had been based, became smaller and continued to diminish decade by decade. Increases in wage earnings rose even more slowly than productivity, so that profits were maintained. The gap between rich and poor widened. Unemployment rates in the industrial countries grew. The prices which the poor ex-colonial countries received for their commodities steadily declined. The gap between their incomes and those of the industrialised countries widened once more, at the same time that inequalities began to open up inside the industrialised countries themselves. What had gone wrong?

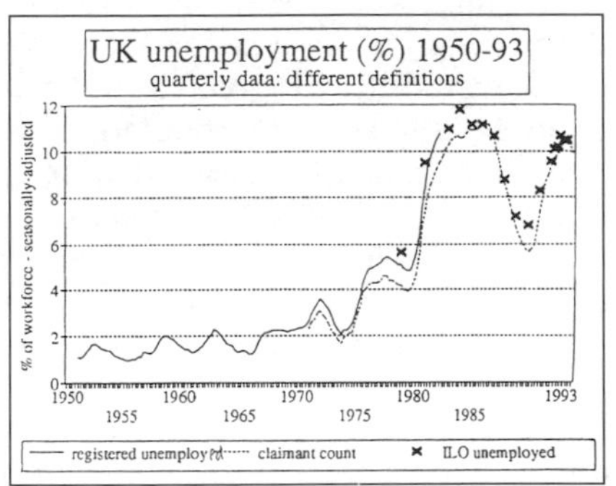

Box 12. Full Employment Policy in the 1950s and 60s.

'... the surge of investment was the significant influence on the high tide of full employment in the 1950s and 1960s. ... What were the conditions that induced the surge of investment? ... The first was the confidence engendered by the full employment policy itself ...the second was that the government set out to encourage it by all manner of special incentives.'

J.R.Sargent for the CLARE Group, *National Institute Economic Review* February, 1995

'Since 1973 ...Much of the rise that occurred in structural unemployment is linked to the slowdown in investment, which in turn is closely linked to restrictive macro-economic policies and deregulation of financial markets.'

UNCTAD, *Trade and Development Report*, 1995, Geneva 1995, p.124

(i) The Money Economy

The problems seemed to lie in the money economy, as we have just seen from the effects of financial liberalisation. The decline can be traced back to 1971 when the United States government ceased to offer gold in exchange for its dollars. Throughout the Nineteenth Century and indeed right up to 1926, while Britain was still the greatest world power, and then from the 1940s when the United States took over, gold provided the standard against which currencies were valued and the reserve for governments to call upon in the last resort to pay their debts. Countries which had reserves of gold could rely on getting credit for their trading activities. World trade expanded. In fact for many years under British hegemony, the £ sterling was as good as gold, because there was an assumption that it could always be exchanged for gold.

After the United States had during the Second World War accumulated most of the world's gold in payment for US war supplies, the same assumption was made, this time that the $ was as good as gold. But during the years after the war the US regularly ran a deficit on its foreign trade and covered it with gold shipments. After 1971, the deficits still mounted up and these were then paid for with dollars. However, nobody worried at first, and a new market opened up for what were called 'Eurodollars', that is for dollars used for payments made outside the US. This helped to finance a great expansion of world trade, and in fact credit grew well ahead of the actual volume of goods traded.

But the United States trade deficits went on growing. Increasingly, these deficits were covered by Japanese lending from the rapidly growing Japanese trade surplus and for some time from the huge surpluses of the oil producing countries. These occurred after the oil producers' cartel, OPEC, hiked the oil price from $1.30 a barrel in the 1960s to $7 in 1973 and $15 in 1977. When the Shah of Persia was ousted, speculation pushed the price up to $40, which encouraged the great expansion of oil production into the North Sea and other oceans, and the price came down to $10 by 1986. It recovered to $20 but is set to fall back to $10 again today. This is a part of the money economy, but it has its effect on the real economy.

Oil drilling in the North Sea.

The real damage done by the 1970s oil price hike was not direct but indirect. Poor countries which imported oil were encouraged to borrow from the oil countries' surplus earnings so as to maintain their purchases. They hoped to be able to pay back from the earnings of their own commodity exports. But, while the price of oil had risen, the prices in world markets of their commodities were falling. Industry was using less raw materials, particularly natural materials, and the industrial countries were subsidising their agricultural production, particularly of substitutes for tropical sugar and vegetable oil.

Rising Interest Rates

At the same time, interest rates rose in the rich countries as the result of their governments' policies, and the poor countries were encouraged to borrow even more to pay the interest on their previous borrowings. They were told by the IMF and the World Bank to pay back by expanding their commodity exports. Since all were told the same thing, there was excess production and commodity prices fell still further. This is the origin of the enormous debts owed by many poor countries particularly in Africa, which have not only held back their development but actually resulted in two decades of declining living standards.

Apart from all the misery and violence that have resulted, this has meant that the purchases of manufactured goods by the commodity producers have been cut back severely. World trade has been to that extent reduced. Jobs in manufacturing industry are lost and we don't actually see our coffee or chocolate getting any cheaper.

The rise in interest rates was a central part of the money economy and

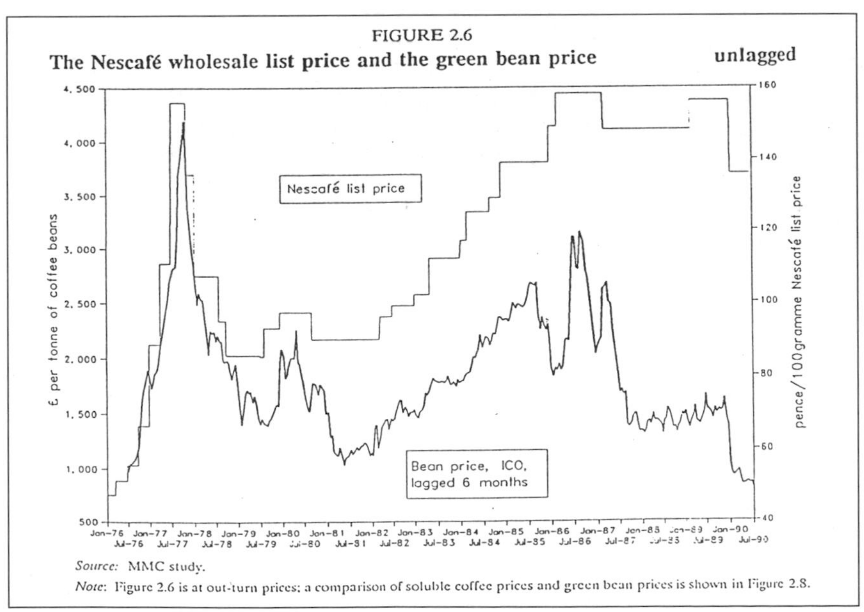

FIGURE 2.6

The Nescafé wholesale list price and the green bean price

Source: MMC study.

Note: Figure 2.6 is at out-turn prices; a comparison of soluble coffee prices and green bean prices is shown in Figure 2.8.

associated with a new emphasis in the policy of governments on protecting the value of money, which came to be called 'monetarism'. We have already seen that raising interest rates was a policy designed by governments to check the growth of the economy and particularly the growth of wage demands and so reduce any subsequent inflationary pressures. Rising oil prices and fast rates of economic growth after the war had undoubtedly resulted in some inflation, and the rate of inflation did increase. For those who had capital this meant some loss, but the value of property rose. Those who had only their wages had to struggle hard to keep these up in line with inflation.

Increasing Power of Capital

Much blame was, therefore, put on the trade unions for supposedly pushing up labour costs in a period of full employment, with all the protection of labour regulation and a strong welfare state. It became accepted government policy to encourage a measure of unemployment and to reduce the protection of labour in order to cut the rate of inflation. The money economists – the so-called 'monetarists' who claim to be pursuing traditional 'neo-classical' policies – argued that the cause of inflation was excess government spending, particularly on measures that maintained full employment.

It was a very convenient argument for the owners of capital who had begun to feel that the powers of trade unions and of labour in general in conditions of full employment were getting too strong and should be curbed. In so far as wages were rising faster than increases in output, they had a point because that would push prices up. But the owners had it in their power to respond. Increases in productivity through the application of new labour saving machinery were in their hands to introduce, and high wages should have encouraged the introduction of such new machinery. The immediate result would be an increase in the reserve army of the unemployed, which was what most employers wished for and which Keynesian measures had been designed to reduce.

In the last resort, if they could not have a labour reserve, owners of capital could move their investment away to places where labour was weaker and wages were lower. This is what they did, and they did all they could to reduce the power of labour and its unions; but the decline in productivity growth went on just the same decade after decade, not only in one or two older industrial sites but almost everywhere. Why did this happen? And what was the impact on those who did have work of the fact that unemployment was higher and economic growth was slower; and how did that connect with the present crisis?

Here is the conclusion of a distinguished American professor, Robert Brenner, who has made the most careful study of movements in the world economy between 1950 and 1998:

Box 13. Capital in Power has Reduced Economic Performance

'Ironically, there has been a very close correlation between the extent to which capital has got its way and the extent to which the performance of the advanced capitalist economies has deteriorated, cycle by cycle since the 1960s. During the 1960s, when ostensibly over-strong labour movements, bloated welfare states, and hyper-regulating governments were at the height of their influence, the global economic boom reached historic peaks. Since then, as the neo-classical medicine has been administered in ever stronger doses, the economy has performed steadily less well. The 1970s were worse than the 1960s, the 1980s worse than the 1970s, and the 1990s have been worse than the 1980s. Speaking only of results and not for the moment of prospects, the long down turn has continued to defy capital's remedies.'

Robert Brenner, 'The Economics of Global Turbulence: A Special Report on the World Economy, 1950-98', *New Left Review*, May-June, 1998, pp.235

(ii) The Real Economy

Monetarist policy errors and movements in the money economy cannot then have been the main origins of the crisis, because the downturn began, as Brenner argues, before the oil price hike and before the monetarists took over government policy-making. What then about the real economy?

Dark satanic mills.

Brenner follows very much the line of thought which Karl Marx was exploring in trying to understand the rising and declining movements of the capitalist economy, especially as he studied it in Britain just over a hundred years ago.

This suggested that the crisis was a crisis of over-production, resulting from a fundamental contradiction in the capitalist system between the accumulation of capital in production and its realisation in the disposal of the extra products. The more profit made for capital from the work of the labourers, the less could they buy back the results of their work and the larger the accumulations of capital the less capable was the capital already invested of self-destruction, renewal and redistribution. It was like Midas in the Greek myth, who turned everything he touched to gold and died because he could not climb over the piles of gold to eat something to sustain him.

Creative Destruction

As more and more production and distribution was taken over by larger and larger transnationally operating companies, these companies came to rely less on competitive strength and more on monopolistic positions. This was just what Marx had foretold, but he recognised also that such centralisation of capital 'in any branch of industry ... would reach its extreme limit if all the individual capitals invested there were fused into a single capital … either in the hands of a single capitalist or a single capitalist company.' Bill Gates's Microsoft offers an extreme example today, but in other branches of industry like the motor car industry, the same process is taking place.

Such monopolists do not need to destroy all old plant, in the 'creative destruction' of surplus capacity, which Joseph Schumpeter had described as 'the genius of capitalism'. This was the process that we saw Robin Murray describing in the closure of Scottish shipyards (Box 6.), which were to be replaced elsewhere by new plant employing fewer workers. The result has been not only the survival (although not in ship-building) of much obsolete plant, but widespread over-production in the culture of an economy that preserves the old, untroubled by competition.

The motor car industry is the most obvious example today. Productivity in the Japanese industry is about three times that in Britain, double that in Germany – as the result mainly of the use of more, and more advanced, machinery. But plants in Europe are protected by a temporary monopoly position and closed down only slowly as companies are taken over or merged and new investment takes place, the latest being the Rover plant in Birmingham threatened with closure by BMW. Preoccupation with financial speculation has reduced still further the incentive to invest.

Box 14. Marx on Capital Accumulation

'The additional capitals formed in the normal course of accumulation serve above all as vehicles for the exploitation of new inventions and discoveries, and industrial improvements in general. But in time the old capital itself reached a point where it has to be renewed in all its aspects, a time when it sheds its skin and is reborn like the other capitals in a perfected technical shape, in which a smaller quantity of labour will suffice to set in motion a larger quantity of machinery and raw material.'

Karl Marx, *Capital*, chapter. 25, section 2.

The current plant closures may then seem inevitable and even desirable. A dynamic economy like that in Korea could make some amends for declining strength elsewhere, but only if general demand was expanding or old production facilities were being abandoned to make room for new. Otherwise, many plants would be working at below capacity. Overall productivity would be held down and costs would rise. It was not then just a matter of the relative strengths of the £ and the *won* that led to the closure of the Korean electronics factories in Britain, but excess capacity world-wide. Without expanding world demand the currency differences only determined where the closures would take place. The system requires 'creative destruction', but how can this be achieved without the destruction also of millions of people's livelihoods in the process, as happened in the 1930s?

The real economy is driven by advancing technology. There have been a succession of major leaps in technological development over the last two centuries, sometimes described as industrial revolutions – in steam power, electrical power, petrol combustion, nuclear power and today in information technology. These have all required radical changes in methods of production and distribution and the scrapping of old plant and investment in new facilities. This is how technology advances, but the scale and cost of new investment are often very great.

When changes are rapid, as they are today, there is a real problem for owners of capital in knowing when to adapt and a strong temptation to hold on to existing investments as long as possible, and a tendency of governments not to do enough to make change easier as the economic cycle develops. This is particularly important in a period of downswing. Governments can even make things worse by cutting back their spending at such a time.

What is the cause of the cycles of boom and slump every few years which have been fairly obviously affecting all industrial countries? Some economists and economic historians have also identified much longer waves of upswing and downturn. How did they come about?

Cycles of Investment

The shorter cycles are generally explained as the result of over-investment in a boom by competing capitalist firms becoming capable of producing beyond the capacity of the market to absorb; this being then followed by a general cut back and the writing off of old plant until production from the new plants and general price cuts create the conditions for a new advance. **But in the boom, as output per worker increases, there is always a widening gap between big increases in profits and small increases in wages. And this must cause demand to fall just as output increases, and to recover only as and when higher productivity is passed on in lower prices. That delay is the cause of the slump.**

The longer cycles are sometimes called 'Kondratieffs' after a Russian economist who first described how they worked in the Nineteenth Century. He noted that on top of the shorter 8-10 year trade cycles of booms and slumps that had been going on ever since the Industrial Revolution there were also since then much longer 50 year cycles with upswings from the 1800s, 1850s and 1900s and downturns from the 1820s and 1870s. They appeared to affect all industrial countries directly and others indirectly and to be associated with the introduction of major technological innovations and these working their way through the economic system. Joseph Schumpeter later described the downturn of the 1930s and upswing of the 1950s on the same basis; but two world wars during those periods had their own impact.

On the Kondratieff pattern of 50 year cycles of capitalist development we were due for another downturn in the 1970s and for a new upturn in the new millennium.

Despite the apparently successful prediction of downturn from the 1970s, there is much argument among economists about the causation and also much uncertainty about the next upturn. For some the role of major wars among rival world powers over a longer period than the last 200 years seems to be most important. Certainly, wars have provided a great stimulus to technical innovation and an equally important demolisher of

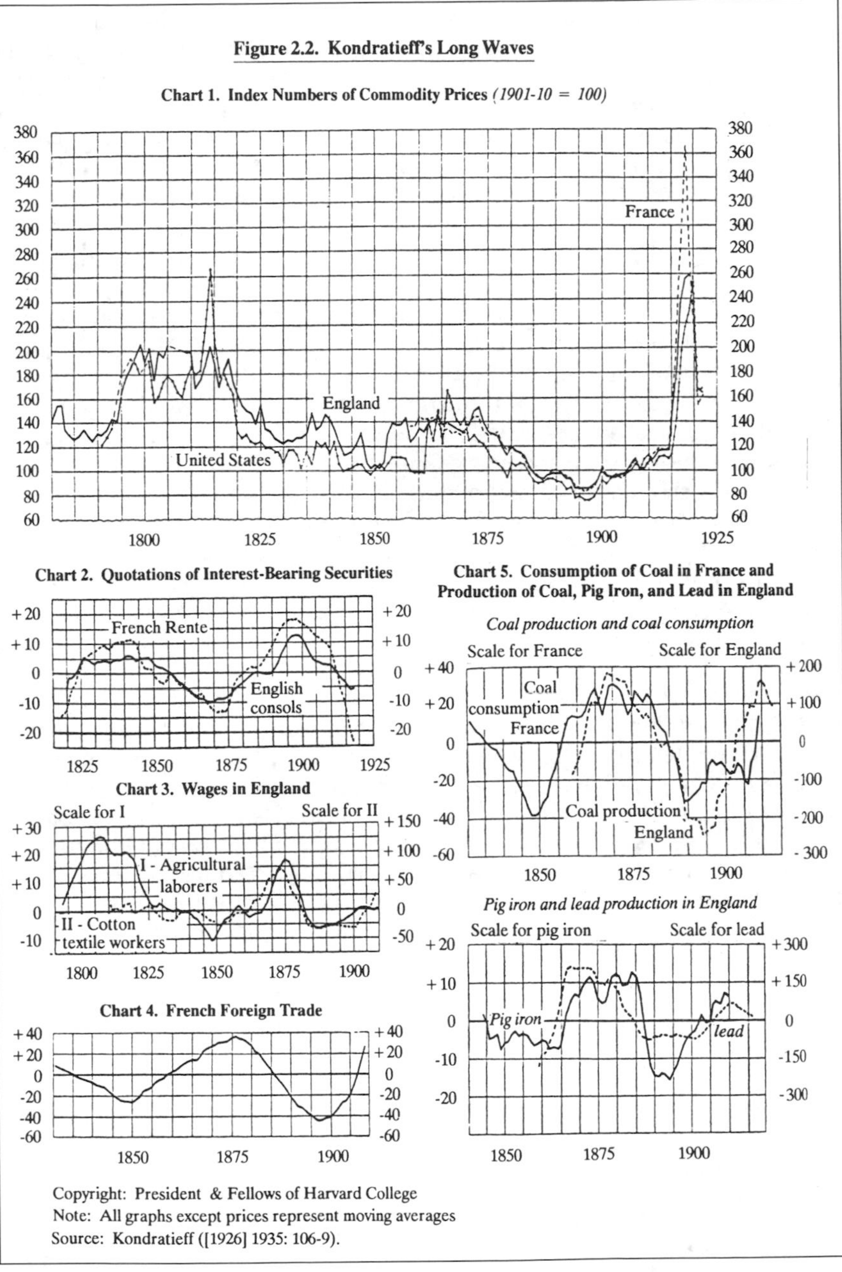

Figure 2.2. Kondratieff's Long Waves

Note: All graphs except prices represent moving averages
Source: Kondratieff ([1926] 1935: 106-9).

earlier productive capacity. This was a major factor in the world-wide recovery after 1945. Given the appalling destructive power of modern weaponry, including the explosion of nuclear devices, a large-scale war today cannot be contemplated.

Nor does it appear that the limits of the revolution in information technology have been reached. In earlier technological revolutions the application of new technology spread steadily outwards from the initial innovating centres, the earliest innovators benefiting most from their temporary monopoly position. This provided some explanation for declining profits and growth rates thereafter, as prices of the new products came down with increasing sales. If innovation today is continuous, the cause of the decline must lie elsewhere, in the manner of the application of the new technology, how it is used and by whom.

Here lies the significance of Professor Brenner's revival of Marx's theory of capitalist overproduction and the absolute necessity for capital to be 'renewed in all its aspects' with 'a smaller quantity of labour and a larger quantity of machinery and raw material'. Destruction of old plant may be much delayed now, and renewal and upturn made more problematic because of the monopoly power of the great companies. But the old must be replaced by the new, if the system is to continue. Unpleasant as it must be, perhaps the present closure of factories everywhere is inevitable under capitalism and even to be welcomed so that we may get on to the next upturn – or change the system?

Since these contradictions occur today on a truly global scale, is there anything that individual governments can do? If my jogging trainers, which were once made in Europe, then in Korea and Indonesia, are now made in China and Vietnam, what can be done not just to protect workers in any of these countries but to ensure some balance between the increasing capacity to produce and the sale of what is produced? If manufacturing is moved always to places where skilled workers are paid less and less, who is to buy what is produced? – not the unemployed workers in Europe, Korea and Indonesia, not certainly the lowest paid of all in China and Vietnam, only the wealthy joggers in the North? But will that be enough? Reducing the price through paying low wages for high skills, using new machinery, may seem to provide a solution for capital, but there must be a long term question about a structural collapse of general demand.

To reach answers to such questions, we have to know more about how the money economy and the real economy interact? Is the present financial crisis a symptom of a much deeper transformation? We have to get that clear, if we are to find reasons for an economic decline that seems to be leading to a deep slump and if we are to make proposals for protecting the great majority of the world's people in that event. First we have to get out of the way some fallacies.

CHAPTER 5

False Assumptions

The chief victim of Professor Brenner's careful study of the last 50 years of capitalist development is the widely held view, now adopted by New Labour, that what is needed to meet current problems of high unemployment is to make people more employable. By more and improved education and training, it is supposed that workers will be able to adapt to the new technology and find employment. But this assumes that the jobs are there and that technology is not going to go on changing and especially in a way that reduces the demand for labour; and this has in fact been the continuous experience of the past several decades. What are known as 'supply side' measures, that is to say making labour more flexible and reducing the regulation of capital, have been consistently applied in nearly all industrialised countries and in many others – with absolutely no beneficial effect on the numbers in employment.

Supply Side Measures Don't Create Jobs

The United States is a special case because at the same time as pursuing such policies of deregulation, successive governments there have increased demand through increased government spending especially on armaments and subsidies to agriculture. And, as we have seen, they have for a long time been able to run a deficit on their trade balance, importing more than they exported, by borrowing from Japan's surplus and other countries' surpluses. The United States could do that where other states would find some difficulty, just because the United States is politically and militarily the most powerful state in the world, and assumed to be always able to repay, because its government issues the world's currency.

The fact is that, if governments decide to deregulate their industries, reduce their public spending at home and expand their exports, there has to be somewhere for the exports to go to. The USA was once this 'somewhere', but this is no longer the case. It was followed by the expanding markets in East Asia, but these are now collapsing. Without some new area of demand, supply side measures in each country simply mean reducing wages and worsening conditions of work to hold on to a share in a world market where demand is everywhere declining. It has been a constantly repeated slogan of New Labour that they will not go back to the old days of 'tax and spend', until by repetition people have come to believe that there is something morally wrong in government taxation and expenditure, which meant some transfer of wealth from rich to poor.

Governments' reliance on supply side measures replaced, as we have seen, a long period of belief in Keynesian demand side measures, that is of 'taxing and spending'. It is necessary to ask why they were ever abandoned. There is a political and an economic answer. Both were suggested by an economist called Kalecki, who proposed similar measures to those of Keynes for dealing with unemployment in the 1930s. Politically, he argued, the growing power of labour under conditions of full employment and with the support of a strong welfare state has the effect of reducing the confidence of capitalists in maintaining their investments. Keynesian measures were therefore on these grounds unacceptable.

The screams of the British employers' organisations at any suggestion of increased state spending on employment and welfare have been enough to force Mr Blair to abandon any commitment he may once have had to full employment. Such protests are, however, not taken so seriously by the large numbers of those who are unemployed or fear unemployment or depend on the state because of sickness, disability or old age. Their voices are not so loud or with such direct access to the media, but with rising unemployment, their strength increases. Overt political repudiation of Keynesian full employment policies would thus hardly be popular in a crisis. When Herr Lafontaine now puts them forward in Germany, he is not attacked on political grounds.

Not Everything was Wrong with Government Spending

It is the economic argument against Keynes which is, therefore, more generally used. This is that Keynesian measures to achieve full employment encourage wage increases and are, therefore, inflationary. This need not be the case if productivity increases are maintained. Indeed rising wages are actually necessary for continuing investment. We saw earlier that in a boom, output per worker tends to grow faster than real earnings. Profits increase and with these come the resources for new investment, but after a time the slow growth of earnings reduces the purchasing power of workers to buy the extra output from the new investment. This we saw to be a main cause of economic crisis, underlying the financial crisis.

Increases in labour productivity can come in different ways: more goods or services may be produced with the same labour, or with more labour but not such a big increase as the increase in output – no problem! but the same volume may be produced with less labour – the problem then arises of reemploying the labour. This is where Keynesian measures of government spending can be applied, to ensure that increases in productivity are maintained, when labour saving machinery is introduced.

UK and EU15:
Annual % Changes in GDP, Productivity, Employment and Earnings, 1961 to 1997

Years	*GDP*		*Productivity*		*Employment*		*Real Earnings*	
	UK	EU15	UK	EU15	UK	EU15	UK	EU15
1961-70	2.9	4.8	2.6	4.6	0.2	0.2	3.0	5.1
1971-80	2.0	3.0	1.7	2.7	0.2	0.3	2.4	3.0
1981-90	2.6	2.4	2.1	1.9	0.6	0.5	2.5	1.1
1991-97	1.6	1.6	2.2	1.9	-0.6	-0.3	0.9	0.8

NOTES: EU15 is the 15 members of the European Union; GDP (national income) is at 1990 market prices; Productivity is GDP per person employed; Employment is occupied population, total economy; Real Earnings are compensation per employee, deflated by price increases in private consumption, total economy.

Against this it is argued that such measures in effect mean government subsidies for industry (agricultural subsidies are not usually mentioned) and these tend to keep in existence plant which is inefficient and should be scrapped, and this overproduction of industrial (and agricultural) capacity both raises prices and lowers rates of profit and checks the growth of productivity. This overproduction is what, according to Professor Brenner, the big companies were perpetrating anyway. If demand had been maintained by government spending, the extra capacity could have been put to use, and the transition to introducing new capacity made easier. But would the working of the capitalist system allow that? We are back to the argument that capital must be free to move where it wants, for it to be used most efficiently. In that case, all government intervention is otiose.

It cannot be, however, that a mixed economy – private and public – is unworkable. When it was practised after the Second World War, it was highly successful, indeed as Professor Brenner has shown, more successful than reliance on the mainly private element in the capitalist economy of today. **It is a false assumption to suppose that government spending necessarily leads to waste and inefficiency.** Not only agriculture but the arms and related aircraft industries still rely heavily in most industrialised countries upon state subsidies, and though they are wasteful of resources in an environmental sense that is not generally held against them and they have the reputation of efficiency in the economic sense of labour productivity.

Much of the privatisation of the last few years in the UK has proved to be very far from efficient. Erstwhile critics of British Rail and of the public Gas, Electricity and Water Boards are having some second thoughts. The most obvious example of inefficiency and waste is the so-called Private Finance Initiative. So as to reduce immediate state spending on capital account, the government in effect borrows money for public works from the private sector, which is then paid back over many years. The payments from the public purse are in the end greater than they would have been and the private financiers have a risk free, state guaranteed income.

It is often said that public enterprise in the Soviet Union was inefficient and wasteful, but the total rebuilding after war-time devastation of major cities like Kiev and Minsk in the space of two decades, complete with libraries, museums, theatres, opera houses and sports stadium, is evidence of the effectiveness of public programmes. The wedding cake architecture may not be to everyone's taste, but the job was done extraordinarily quickly.

There is other evidence. The Belo-Russian grain harvest has survived the Soviet collapse. We may forget that Yuri Gagarin was the first cosmonaut, but can remember that his US successors were all involved in a *state* financed programme. It is a little recognised fact, indeed, that in the United States it was federal public agencies that were also the main sources of the development of silicon chips, super-computers and information technology generally, leading to the initiation of the Internet.

As the earlier quotation from Professor Brenner reminded us, it was the years of Keynesian full employment policies, supported by high government spending and a strong welfare state, that were the years of economic boom everywhere. Subsequent years of monetarist policies have been years of much reduced economic growth. **It was only US government spending on arms and agriculture that sustained the American market for so long and reports by World Bank economists have begun increasingly to recognise that the dynamic economies of East Asia were the result of far more state intervention at an early period in their development than had been previously allowed for.**

Too Little Regulation, Not Too Much

It is, however, a further false assumption to claim that the recent economic collapse in East Asia and in Russia was caused by too much continuing intervention by governments, and that what is required is further economic reform. That is to say, still more freedom for the owners of capital to move their money where they like without consideration for the needs of the people involved or the general stability of the system.

On the contrary, as we have seen, the crises in Asian countries and in Russia are the direct result of *reduced* government action to redistribute incomes from the rich to the poor and of inadequate regulation by government of investments by the banks and others, including speculative property investments, and of the unscrupulous and often corrupt private transfers of assets out of

these countries into Swiss bank accounts and other tax havens. Government deregulation has left the whole world economy open to panic behaviour in the financial markets, with no support in the last resort from the International Financial Institutions, although this was supposed to be the role of the IMF.

Box 15. Financial Panics

'In a world of extreme exchange rate variability, panics threaten whole countries, not just financial institutions within them...Suppose that foreign investors become substantially more risk averse, perhaps for reasons that have little to do with the country. Such herd behaviour may drive a government into default, companies into bankruptcy and a country into depression, quite unnecessarily.'

Martin Wolf 'The Last Resort', *Financial Times*, 23.09.98

Deregulation affects not only capital movements but company taxation. The avoidance of tax is a main activity of the finance directors of large companies. Those that operate transnationally are able to establish offices in Switzerland and Lichtenstein and on offshore islands like the Bahamas, where not only are taxes low but accounts can be filed without being made public. What these companies do is to operate a system of transfer pricing, so that as much as possible of the profits made throughout their empires appears to be made in the country with the lowest tax levels and the minimum requirements of transparency, and tax is thus avoided in the

countries with high taxation. Worse than this, the real value of commodities produced and of equipment supplied can be concealed by transfer pricing from the governments of the countries where production takes place.

Tragically it often happens that the governments concerned are caught up in the corruption of the whole business. Since ministers get their own rake-off, they tend not to ask questions. The bribes that they receive enable them not only to salt funds away in Swiss bank accounts, but to reward their local clientele of hangers on and bodyguards. Anyone who blows the whistle will find themselves not only deprived of perquisites but threatened with legal proceedings and even with their lives endangered. The Ogoni people in Nigeria protesting against the operations of a major oil company suffered the ultimate penalty.

Box 16. Transfer Pricing by the Transnational Companies

It has been estimated by an expert who worked for the UN Centre for Transnational Companies that, if the transnational mining companies had paid the full world market value for the minerals they extracted from Africa between 1975 and 1995, the foreign debt of African governments which accumulated during these years to over $200 billions, requiring some 25% of their export earnings to service each year, would never have accumulated at all.

Quoted in Michael Barratt Brown & Pauline Tiffen, *Short Changed: Africa and World Trade*, Pluto Press, 1993

Freedom for Capital Does Not Benefit Everyone

The most dangerous false assumption about capitalism is that free trade and the free movement of capital benefit all parties. Using different metaphors – that wealth trickles down and that a rising tide raises all boats – it is assumed that the growth of income world wide is equally shared. It is not. The trickle dries up. Some boats are holed, others cannot carry the weight of passengers in them and few can weather the storms at sea like the ocean liners. This is not just bad luck; it is built into the system. The facts are there for all to see. The gap between the rich and the poor has been widening steadily for thirty years, not only between rich and poor countries but inside both. Unless action is taken by governments to correct the tendency, capital accumulation generates wealth at one pole and poverty at the other.

This polarisation is not only the result of the abuse of transfer pricing or of any other non-economic methods of exploitation. It is the result of the very process of accumulation, which lies at the heart of the system. Profit can be realised for *some* capital from monopoly positions established in the market, but the profit for *all* capitals in competition must come from paying labour less than the value of what labour produces. If all of the difference is reinvested in new production and new employment, then there may be big differences in the rewards of those involved, but inequalities will not necessarily grow. If, however, unemployment arises because of technical change or the spread of new technologies, and labour is not re-employed, or is re-employed at a lower wage, then inequalities will grow. This is what has been happening.

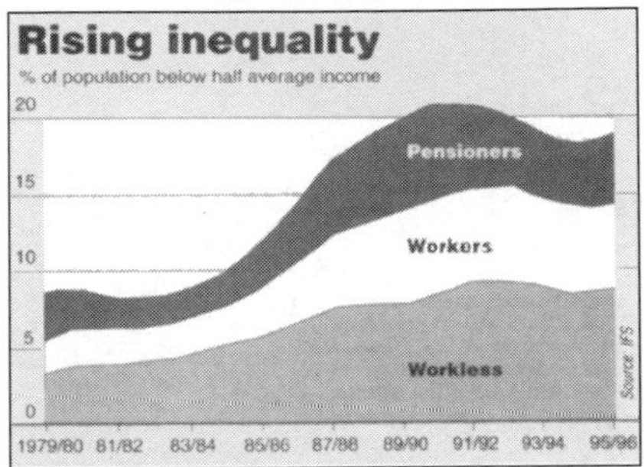

Box 17. The Rich get Richer; the Poor get Poorer

'In the 25 years up to 1995 the industrial countries with about 900 million people recorded a 2.3% annual increase in consumption of goods and services. The same number of people in Africa and the Middle East actually consumed 20% less over the same period... [This was partly the result of faster population growth, but] the total increase in consumption of the industrial countries was $16,500 billions, while that in Africa and the Middle East was only $500 billions.'

UN Development Programme (UNDP), *Human Development Report*, 1998

It is true that new countries, especially in East Asia, have been added to the list of industrialised countries in this period and there have been improvements for many people in the non-industrialised countries – in literacy, infant mortality and life expectancy – but the gap between the poorest 20% and the richest 20% has widened. The richest countries now account for 86% of all consumption and the poorest for just 1.3%. Such inequalities have grown wider also *inside* the industrial countries. A proportion of their populations, varying from 7% to 17%, according to the UNDP Report, has been excluded from progress – in longevity, education and a decent living standard. The USA ranks first in average income but registers the highest human poverty of the industrialised countries.

In the decade between 1979 and 1990, when US economic growth was fastest, Professor Brenner reported the lack of any advantage for wage workers in the US,

> 'annual hourly real wages and salaries (excluding benefits) actually falling ... at an average annual rate of 1% and for the bottom 80% continuing to fall thereafter.'

At the other extreme the wealth of a few continues to grow.

Box 18. The Billionaires

'225 individual billionaires in the world [60 of them in the USA], are estimated to have assets equal to the combined annual incomes of the poorest 47% of the world's people, that is 2.5 billion people. The three richest of them have assets that exceed the yearly income of the 48 least developed countries.'

UNDP Human Development Report, 1998, New York 1998

And this was not only happening in the USA. The gap between rich and poor was also widening in the UK. The latest figures from the Department of Social Security show that between 1979 and 1995-7, average incomes after housing costs increased in real terms by 44%, but the top tenth of households enjoyed a rise of 70%, while the bottom tenth suffered a cut of 9%.

It is hard to understand how this situation has come to be tolerated, but it is not simply a moral question of a monstrous social injustice. **It is also an economic disaster; this accumulation of wealth at one pole and of poverty at the other means that capital ceases to be invested productively because the workers have not the wherewithal to purchase the products of new and ever more labour saving investment. This is the fatal flaw in the system of capitalist accumulation.**

The contrasts between wealth and poverty can be put in a very positive way, as the UNDP 1998 Report reveals:

Box 19. A 4% Tax on the Super Rich

'It is estimated that the additional cost of achieving and maintaining universal access to basic education for all, basic health care for all, reproductive health care for all women, adequate food for all and safe water and sanitation for all is roughly $40 billion a year. This is less than 4% of the combined wealth of the 225 richest people in the world'.

UNDP *Human Development Report 1998*, New York 1998, p.30

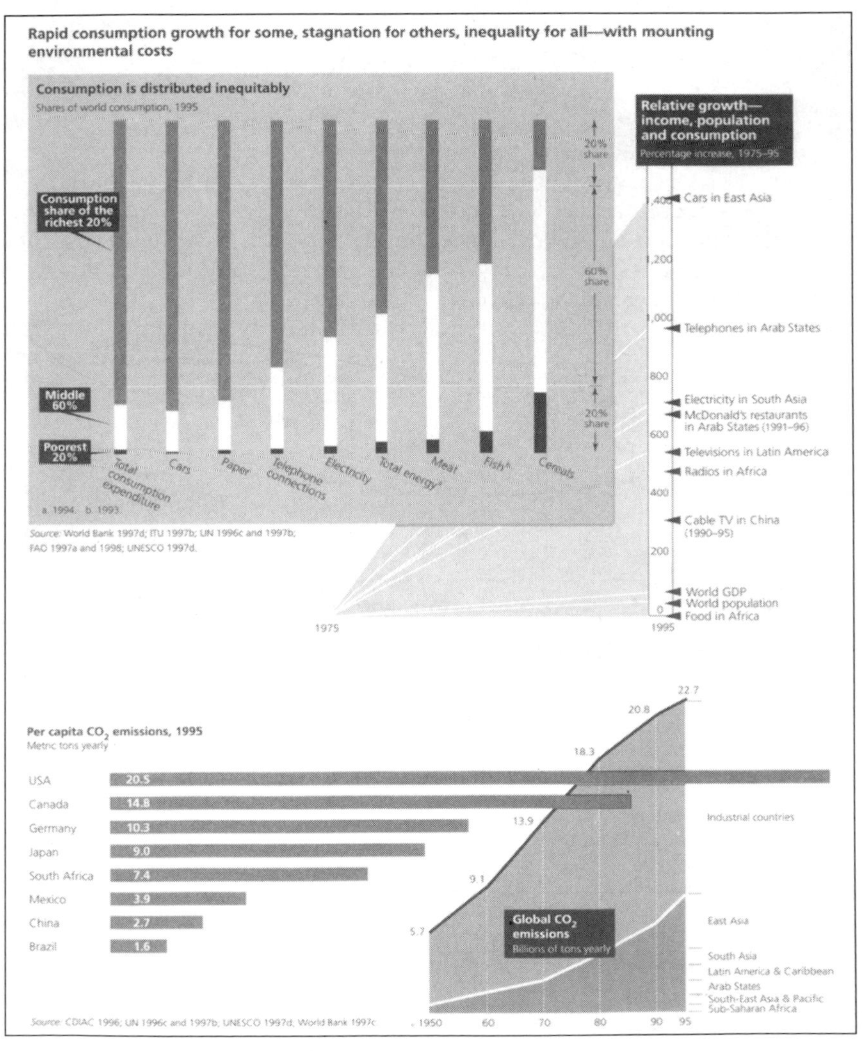

Humanity cannot afford to tolerate such inequalities. They offend against both human justice and economic stability. It cannot be beyond the wit of politicians to find a way to tax such wealth – at the modest rate of 4% a year – to provide the basis of a decent life for all.

And the Earth Can't Take it

All this capital accumulation is made far worse by the fact that the rich not only consume most of the world's resources – 20% of the people account for 85% of total consumption; it was only 70% in 1965 – but they account for over 90% of the impact on the environment, North America and Western Europe alone contributing 60% to global warming. It has been calculated that five earth planets would be required to process the carbon dioxide emissions if all countries were to equal those of a rich western European country like Germany. These figures are taken from the report of the UN Development Programme on Human Development for 1998, which seeks to show the fatal connection between inequality and environmental destruction.

It is not just in Germany that reds and greens can unite, although it is there that they have shown the way – in actual government.

It is a false assumption, regrettably accepted by many governments including New Labour, that deregulation of environmental controls like cheap labour is necessary to attract employers to create jobs. The external costs have to be paid for in the end, but they are, of course, paid by society and not by the employer. The polluter doesn't pay. There is a further argument against deregulation, even on grounds of international competitiveness, and that is that the failure to develop clean technology forfeits the lead in a growth market.

Box 20. The Double Dividend: Jobs and the Environment

'We must avoid the false argument that environmental protection and job creation are incompatible. Both experience and research have shown that the two are linked in the medium term and inseparable in the long term… the environmental sector already employs 1.5 million people in the European Union. Over the last ten years, the proportion of people employed in that sector has grown twice as fast as the total working population.'

Jacques Delors, 'Development: A New Model', a paper prepared in 1996 for the Party of European Socialists (published in *European Labour Forum*, no.18,winter 1996/7)

Most of the increase in labour productivity over the last few decades has been the result of substituting fossil fuel energy for human energy. The result has been not only the rapid depletion of natural resources but damage to the environment, both by pollution of land, air and water and by global warming and destruction of the ozone layer. Yet, labour continues to be heavily taxed, without much redistribution between rich and poor, and fossil fuels are neither assessed at their true value, nor protected against exploitation. Petrol consumption by motorists may seem to be quite heavily taxed, at least in Europe, not in the United States, but petroleum products are actually subsidised in their use in agriculture and some other industries.

The aim of reducing the taxes on labour, both income tax and social insurance contributions, has in recent years attracted many governments, including those with a socialist orientation. Indirect taxes on sales like VAT have in part taken the place of direct taxes. The result has been to discriminate in favour of the rich who previously paid more of their income in direct taxes than the poor, but also in another way against the poor who spend more of their incomes on VAT rated goods than the rich do. The detailed results of the tax changes in the UK between 1977 and 1996 are shown in Michael Barratt Brown, *Defending the Welfare State*, (Spokesman for Independent Labour Network, 1998, p.82, Table 6.)

An alternative tax, which is strongly favoured by the Greens, is a tax on carbon dioxide emissions. This would not only have the effect of reducing pollution and the depletion of scarce resources, but of encouraging the

Table 6
UK Taxes and Benefits of Households:
By Income Group in Quintiles, 1995-6 with a comparison of 1977

A. Original Income and Gross Income (£s) and Taxes						
Income Group	*Bottom*	*4th*	*3rd*	*2nd*	*Top*	*All*
Original Income	2,430	6,090	13,790	22,450	41,260	17,200
Cash Benefits	4,910	4,660	3,360	2,130	1,190	3,250
Gross Income	7,340	10,750	17,150	24,580	42,450	20,450
All Taxes	3,060	3,860	6,420	9,270	15,560	7,640
Post-Tax Income	4,280	6,890	10,730	15,310	26,890	12,820
B. Taxes/Benefits % of Original Income						
Direct Taxes and NIC	46	25	23	23	25	25
Indirect taxes	79	34	34	18	12	20
Total Taxes	125	59	57	41	37	45
Cash Benefits	205	80	25	9	3	23
Benefits in Kind	162	55	23	12	5.5	18
C. Taxes as % of						
Gross Income 1995	41.5	36	37.5	37.5	36.6	37.5
Gross Income 1977	28	36	35.5	35.5	36.5	35

Sources: for 1995/6: 'Effects of Taxes and Benefits upon Household Income, 1995-6', *Economic Trends*, March 1997, p.29; for 1977: *Economic Trends*, January 1979

development of clean technologies. Such a tax need not constitute a handicap in international competition, but could, in Jacques Delors's phrase, pay 'a double dividend: less pollution and more employment'. It is a matter of changing the direction of technology to meet human needs and protect the planet.

Box 21. The Upper and the Lower Limits of Wealth Creation

'Technical progress provides us with a floor under which nobody has to fall. Scarcity can be removed. The hope of socialism is that all people can live a dignified life. Environmentalism adds another dimension. It says there is not just a lower limit [for human survival], there is also an upper limit. There is a threshold beyond which there can be no more justice or democracy because progress, or wealth creation, takes a form in which not everyone can participate. There is a ceiling. If you go beyond it, wealth creation becomes oligarchic in nature.'

Wolfgang Sachs, German Green, interviewed in *New Internationalist*, ed. David Ransom, November 1998.

A sobering fact for those who believe in an extended role for the state appears in the UNDP report for 1998, that in the early 1990s governments were subsidising environmentally damaging industrial activities – energy, water, roads, agriculture – world-wide to the tune of $710 billions a year, 14 times what is required to eradicate absolute poverty. Switching even a part of those expenditures from destruction to poverty alleviation would thus have a double benefit for mankind. How could this be done?

Venice sinking.

Part Two

What Could Be Done About It

CHAPTER 6

National Action

While the world economy has been marked by steady growth for some decades, this has been at a decreasing rate, and inequalities have also been growing. It should not be assumed, however, that economic growth is only possible where inequalities develop. The UNDP Report for 1997 showed that inequalities are greatest inside the poorest countries and argued that a reduction in poverty and the establishment of greater equality encourages growth – through better health and more education and generally greater preparedness to take risks and engage in new enterprise. This, the Report then argued, means strong government action to maintain demand.

More especially, greater equality implies an expansion of purchasing power, which creates the demand for new production and new investment. There are narrow limits to the consumption of the 225 billionaires, even with all their houses and yachts. Their great wealth has somehow to be set to work to make more money, if it is not to be eroded, and that means setting people to work to produce goods and services for which there has to be a growing demand. And there is the nub of the matter.

The accumulation of such wealth has taken place out of the exploitation of men and women who are thereby left with reduced purchasing power, and the small number of these giant accumulations of capital means more reliance on monopoly positions, less competition, more overproduction, less reinvestment, more unemployment. It is a vicious circle, unless broken into by government intervention. **For, what the Keynesian measures were doing that maintained full employment for thirty years after the Second World War was to redistribute income from the savings of the rich to the spending of the poor, as well as to regulate capital movements.**

Must Full Employment Mean Inflation?

This last statement indicates the basic thrust of the policies required both to ease the suffering resulting from the current crisis and to prevent it from deepening and continuing. Keynesian policies are often derided by New Labour as 'tax and spend' and 'throwing money at a problem', which supposedly had little effect on the actual position of the poor. The new vogue word is 'targeting', which really means separating out the very poorest from the not so poor by means testing. This is both administratively costly and humiliating. It is combined in Mr Brown's economics with stability, which means preserving the value of money – for those who have it. And the pursuit of this aim has resulted as we have seen, not in all benefiting but in the poor getting poorer.

Keynesian policies were also targeted; it was the rich who were taxed; and the spending, the 'money thrown', was at all those who were unemployed or sick or beyond working age and at parts of the country where these disabilities were concentrated. There is certainly room for more precision in identifying the areas of greatest deprivation from industrial closures and subsequent unemployment. The statistical information on conditions in individual districts in Britain is grossly inadequate as the result of manpower cuts in the statistical services, and the right answer to this is not to have more staff engaged on the means testing of individuals.

It is said by the monetarists that too much public spending causes prices to rise, but such inflationary pressure is far from necessarily true when there is unused capacity in the economy. Most economists now agree that there is no such thing as what the monetarists call a universal 'Non-Accelerating Inflationary Rate of Unemployment (NAIRU)', such as makes them believe that an economy must always have some unemployment to stop the inflation rate accelerating. It all depends on the state of the economy. There is a danger of inflationary price increases if there is a large gap between the rise in workers' earnings and the increase in productive capacity to meet their demands. But there is little sign of any such gap opening up today, except where there are special problems of industrial collapse as in Russia. Rather the opposite is the case. There is, as we have seen, world-wide *over*-production.

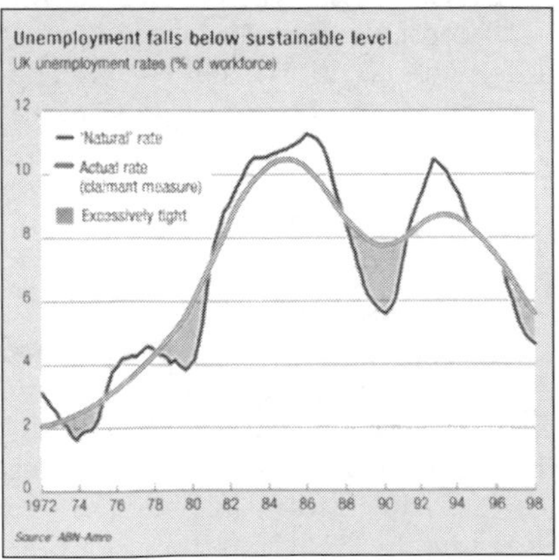

The problem today for the governments of each of the industrialised countries is seen by them to be to maintain the competitiveness in world markets of the industries located in their countries. We have seen how the transnational companies shift their production around the world according to changes in local labour costs, capital regulations and currency values. But deflationary policies, keeping labour costs down, deregulating capital and devaluing the currency provide only one way of remaining competitive and a rather short-term way, unless at the same time investment is maintained in productive capacity.

If economies are not already buoyant – and the situation in 1999 is that they are not; almost all are being cut back by government in the hope that someone else will take their exports – it is positive government action that is required to support productive investment either directly or with aid to industry or by other means to sustain demand. But this can only be achieved by redistributing income from the rich savers to the poor spenders. And it cannot be done in one country alone.

There is a nice story of a meeting of European finance ministers when each in turn declared their sincere intention to follow the bankers' advice and moderate the pressure of demand in their economies and achieve a foreign trade surplus so as to control inflation. The representative of Norway was the last to speak and he said that he was very touched by the confidence shown in the Norwegian economy, but he had to tell them that it could not absorb all the others' surpluses.

It is not being argued here that the first alternative to such policies of deflation is necessarily inflation, but it has to be expansion of demand where there are high rates of unemployment, and that means particularly in areas where such rates are highest.

Will Lowering Interest Rates Create Jobs?

The only proposal that the leading industrial economies have agreed on in order to stem the gathering downturn of their economies is to reduce interest rates. This may have some beneficial effects. Some firms and governments will feel able to increase their borrowing to expand investment in projects which might lead to higher employment. Many families will feel able to spend more because their mortgage payments are reduced and even to take out a mortgage which they had not previously been able to afford. There will be a generally more optimistic view among businessmen about future demand which may lead them to start new job creating projects and to maintain existing ones.

But there are three difficulties: the first is that interest rates in different countries vary. They vary, as we have seen, according to the confidence that investors world-wide have in any country's economic prospects and stage of recovery. A country with an economy that investors distrust, especially if its currency is expected to be devalued in the near future, will have to offer higher rates of interest to persuade those with money to leave their money in that country. We have already noted how a poor country like Ghana has a very high interest rate regime, while a rich country like Switzerland always has very low rates. This means that the poverty of the one and the wealth of the other become cumulative: Swiss businessmen can

borrow much more cheaply than Ghanaians, among other advantages, so that their products are more competitive in world markets. Thus agreement among the most industrialised countries' governments to reduce interest rates, even if it can be reached, will not help the poorer countries, even among those that are industrialised, let alone among the poorest.

The second difficulty is that the effect of interest rates will be different in different parts of any large country. This was made clear by the Governor of the Bank of England who recently declared that some unemployment in the North of the UK was a price worth paying for controlling inflation in the South. My grandfather, who was a Lancashireman, used to say that 'brass is made in't North and spent in't South.' There is still some truth in the adage, in that much manufacturing takes place in the North and many of the rich living on unearned income are to be found in the South. Rising incomes among those living in the South may be said to be pushing up prices. So, it is argued that interest rates must not be lowered too much, even though this still leaves difficulties for manufacturing in the North.

It will be even truer of different parts of the European Union, with much more disparate regional conditions, if under EMU the bankers from the richer parts seek to keep down inflation by holding interest rates high. The parts where industry is located, and especially where it has been located in the past and closed down, as the British coalfields have been, will need much lower rates, if they are to be assisted and not actually to suffer from further unemployment. Otherwise, people like Graham Jones (see Box 1.) will stay unemployed.

The third difficulty with lowering interest rates as a stimulus for generating employment through private investment is the most serious.

Since the new technology in both goods and service industries tends to be labour saving, there is no guarantee that there will be any new jobs created as a result of private investment encouraged by lower interest rates; nor that these new jobs will be created in areas of high unemployment. Existing inequalities in the distribution of income will not be corrected, so that the central cause of the crisis will not be addressed.

This is the limitation of all supply side answers to the crisis.

Box 22. An Activist State to Enable the Poor

'A poverty eradication strategy requires not a retreating weak state but an active, strong one, and that strength should be used to enable the poor rather than disable them.'

UNDP, *Human Development Report*, 1997, p.101

It Needs Governments to Generate Employment

It is only public spending by governments that can ensure that investment results in generating new jobs and in the areas where they are most needed. This is perhaps such an important point that it should be repeated. Keynes used to say as a joke that it did not matter what governments spent their money on so long as it created employment where there was unemployment; they could build pyramids if they so wished. But the fact is that there are great needs for building work, short of pyramids (or domes), to make up for many years of neglect and environmental destruction. There is a special need for investment in housing insulation and other forms of resource saving and in environmental protection and clearing up of pollution – all highly labour intensive activities.

Studies of the high levels of unemployment in the communities where coal mining has been terminated have shown that local authorities had any number of projects pigeon-holed for lack of funds. Recent announcements of special funding in Britain for local government relate to measures which are no more than repeating the rescue operations of previous years, combined with much more hype about combating social exclusion. Cleaning up the countries' worst housing estates is an admirable aim, but the sum proposed for local government spending of £800 million over five years, while it sounds large, is in fact derisory. The latest estimate of the cost of creating one new job is £10,000, even taking into account the social security saved and the take up in taxation. If that figure is correct, 80,000 new jobs would be created, if all the money were spent on job creation. Much of it will in fact be needed for building and other materials.

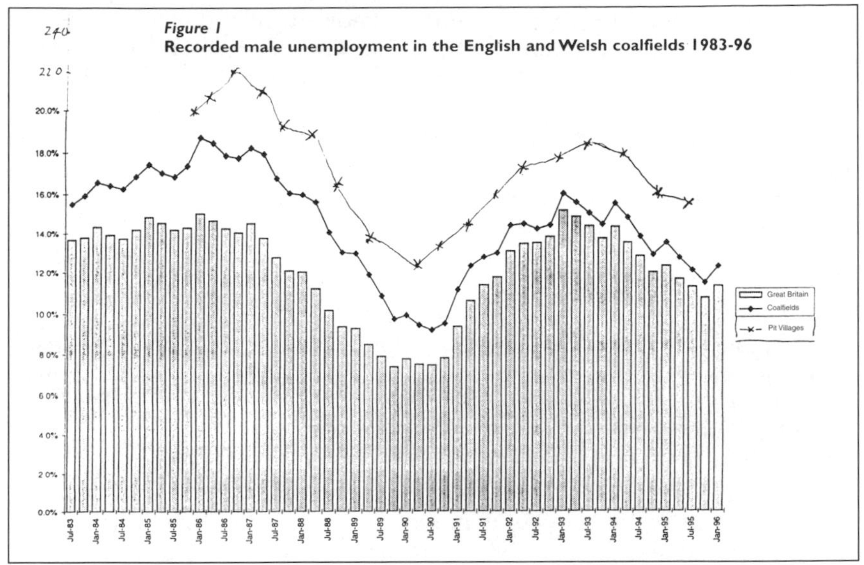

Figure I
Recorded male unemployment in the English and Welsh coalfields 1983-96

Box 23. Unemployment – Short-term and Long-term, All the Same

'This focus [by New Labour] on the reduction of long-term unemployment is indicative of 'new monetarism', as it sees long term unemployment as eroding skills and the work ethic, loosening ties with the labour market, but also not having an inflationary impact. Thus long term unemployment can be reduced without risking inflation, but not short-term unemployment.'

Philip Arestis & Malcolm Sawyer, 'New Labour, New Monetarism', in *Soundings*, no.9, Summer, 1998

The areas that are suffering from unemployment extend far beyond the most deprived estates. The coalfield communities affected by high unemployment, for example, have populations of about one million men and women of working age, one half of whom report themselves to be desirous of working if work were available. What chance do they have of finding it? Mrs Beckett, a previous New Labour Secretary of State for Trade and Industry, made it clear that there was no more public money for coalfield communities. They would have to depend on private industry. But without state aid what chance have these areas of attracting private investment?

Private capital is rarely invested today in large projects unless there has been some sweetener from the state, and the infrastructure of roads, electricity and gas supplies, water, sewerage and even housing and schools has to be supplied by the state for any new development. This is just another argument for public enterprise and against private finance initiatives. Why should we pay to make the private financiers rich?

Taxing the Rich to Help the Poor

Mr Gordon Brown, as Chancellor of the Exchequer, has announced an increase in public expenditure in real terms of 3% a year from 1999 to 2001. This is to be welcomed, but in spite of all the hype, it will not bring the proportion of public spending in the national income back to the level obtaining in 1996 (after the 1997 cuts the proportion fell from 41.2% of GDP to 39.5%, and is now to be brought up to 40.5% by 2001). It should be brought back all the way, at least to the 1996 level, if it is to check rising unemployment. But any such increase was clearly ruled out by Mr Blair at the 1998 TUC, and the ruling was repeated very firmly by Mr Brown at the 1998 Labour Party Conference, although subsequent recognition of the threat of slump has begun to make him less categorical.

The fact is that such moneys cannot be found without raising taxes, which Mr Blair has rejected in deference to his so-called 'Middle England' middle class voters. It is not widely recognised just how much the richer groups in Britain have benefited from the tax changes under Conservative governments from 1980 onwards. In 1977 the top 20% of income earners were paying a somewhat larger proportion of their incomes in taxes than the average earner and a much larger proportion than the bottom 20%. By 1995 they were paying a smaller proportion than any of the other groups and very much smaller than the lowest group, whose tax take had gone up from 28% to a monstrous 41.5% (see table on page 49). Mr Brown's 1998 budget was aimed to reduce this last figure, without increasing what is called the 'burden' on the rich. But over 20 years the incomes of the top 20% have risen to ten times those of the bottom 20% – a greater degree of inequality than in any other European country except Switzerland.

Introducing a new tax band into UK income assessments of 55% after £40,000 a year of personal income would yield £6 billion. The rate of tax could be raised still higher on the highest incomes, those of the 'fat cats' – back nearer to the levels of the 1960s and 70s – so as to find the same sums without such a high rate for those on £40,000 to £50,000. To raise the higher rates and get the same yield, it would be necessary greatly to strengthen the measures for controlling the tax avoidance dodges of banking in the Channel Islands, the Isle of Man and elsewhere. The sums involved in such tax havens are estimated as the equivalent of the whole British annual national income. Even a small increase of taxation on such sums would yield an enormous income. But some more members of the Government might have to resign.

In addition, the upper limit for National Insurance contributions could be raised to find further sums for Old Age Pensioners, who are amongst the poorest groups in British society. The subsidies which are now provided for those on higher incomes through mortgage relief, private education and health could be reduced or eliminated, if a real attempt was made to restore the much greater state of equality in the UK during the decades after the Second World War. But this would imply a major educational campaign to re-educate 'Middle England' to understand the advantages for all in a more egalitarian society.

The UN Development Programme (UNDP) *Human Development Report* has already been quoted, arguing that inequalities discourage growth as well as causing unacceptable levels of poverty. The International Labour Office (ILO) has added its voice, representative of governments, employers and trade unions, arguing that the Asian financial crisis has **'shown the cost of neglecting social concerns'** and warning that one third of the world's 3 billion workers will be either without a job or under-employed by next year with the growing global crisis. Is this also a 'price worth paying' to preserve the value of money?

Box 24. On Not Neglecting Social Concerns

'The pace of globalisation has been primarily driven by market forces, and national and to some extent international rules, institutions and practices needed to render its consequences socially acceptable have been insufficiently developed.'

International Labour Office, *World Labour Report*, 1998-99

The central argument of this book has been that the world crisis is a crisis of unequal development. **The neglect of social concerns is not just a moral question, but an economic problem.** The tendency in capitalism to polarise wealth and poverty must, if it continues, become in the end self-defeating. But correcting this tendency requires government action and cannot be effected on a national basis only. International action is required, and it will have to go beyond remedial measures, to have any countervailing influence on the in-built tendencies of the capitalist system.

CHAPTER 7

International Action

To deal with a world crisis, it cannot be enough to step up public spending in one country. To bring down unemployment in Europe and world-wide, common action is required. This was proposed by Jacques Delors when he was the President of the European Commission. His proposal was to use the powers of the European financial institutions, in the same way as the federal budget of the United States, to offset the cuts in each Member State's national public spending which were being made in order to meet the very strict monetary criteria set by the Maastricht Agreement for entry into the European Economic and Monetary Union. Common action under the Delors proposal was to support infrastructural developments of rail links, to increase structural funds for the poorer regions and to finance SMEs (Small and Medium Enterprises which tend to create more jobs than the giant companies), without offending against the Maastricht Agreement.

The Delors target was 15 million new jobs by the year 2000. The proposal has been steadily watered down in the name of monetary stability and in the fear of federalism, until today practically nothing remains. It is as if in the 1930s President Roosevelt in the United States had been deprived of all federal power, on top of whatever the separate states were doing, to create jobs under the New Deal to offset the Great Depression. Without that power there would have been no Tennessee Valley Authority and the whole system of flood control and power generation in the great Mississippi-Missouri rivers of the United States would not exist, and US unemployment would have been heavier and more prolonged.

There is new hope, however, for the Delors Plan now from the new governments elected recently in France, Germany and Italy. All have indicated at the European Union summit meeting in Austria that they are prepared to go back to these proposals. The English advocates of the Delors Plan, who won support for it in the European Parliament in the Coates Committee Report on Full Employment, and have since been rubbished by Mr Blair, are exonerated. They are still being denounced by those whom Martin Wolf of the *Financial Times* calls the 'obdurate bankers' but he warns them that they will have now to take account of 'politicians who care about employment and growth.'

Bangladeshis waiting for food relief.

Cancelling the Poor Countries' Debts and Ending the Rich Countries' Protection

European measures are still not enough to offset what is a world crisis. Once again the aim must be to correct the growing inequalities of income world-wide. A start would be to cancel the debts of the poorest countries, mainly in Africa. These we saw were originally incurred during the oil price hike, but have steadily accumulated since through further borrowing to pay the interest on past borrowings. Thus the original creditors or their successors have got their money back many times over. Cancelling these debts has been much talked about, but never achieved. Where serious discussions have been begun, as with the government of Uganda, whose views we quoted earlier, the International Financial Institutions – the World Bank and the IMF – have imposed conditions requiring public spending cuts which were entirely counter productive of increased employment and improved living standards.

The sums of money involved for cancelling the foreign debts of the poorest countries are relatively small, much less than the governments of the industrialised countries have already found to ease the debts of the banks in their own countries. These banks had become involved in lending to developing countries, and were allowed by governments in the rich countries to class these debts as losses for tax purposes, although they had not been written off. This easement was not, therefore, passed on to the poor countries themselves, but was of course paid for by tax payers in the rich countries.

The devastating hurricane that struck Central America in October 1998 has aroused some concern in the rich countries about the debt payments,

which the poor countries of Central America have to make to the rich. It has been proposed by Gordon Brown for the British Government that, because of the hurricane damage, these payments should be 'put on hold', while the countries concerned rebuild their shattered towns and villages. It is not proposed that they should be cancelled and other countries have yet to agree. This is in stark contrast to the immediate rescue by the US and other governments of Long Term Capital Management (LTCM), a hedge fund of the super rich, to the tune of a sum equal to all the debts of the Central American states added together.

Beyond debt cancellation, a new fund is required for targeting social deprivation, not by means tests but by public investment in specific health and education and housing projects along lines already laid down by the UN Development Programme, to eradicate overall poverty within two decades. Programmes would encourage self-help among groups of women and young people, through the provision of funds for local development. This can only be done by taxing the rich chiefly in the rich countries; and there is much resistance to any such idea. One proposal which might be more widely acceptable is a tax on speculation. This is the idea of a Nobel prize-winning economist, Professor Tobin. We have already seen the damaging effects of financial speculation in world markets, so that we can expect that this tax would be killing two birds with one stone.

The debt payments are only one aspect of the unequal relations between the industrialised countries and the poorest countries of the Third World. We have already noted the abuse of transfer pricing by transnational

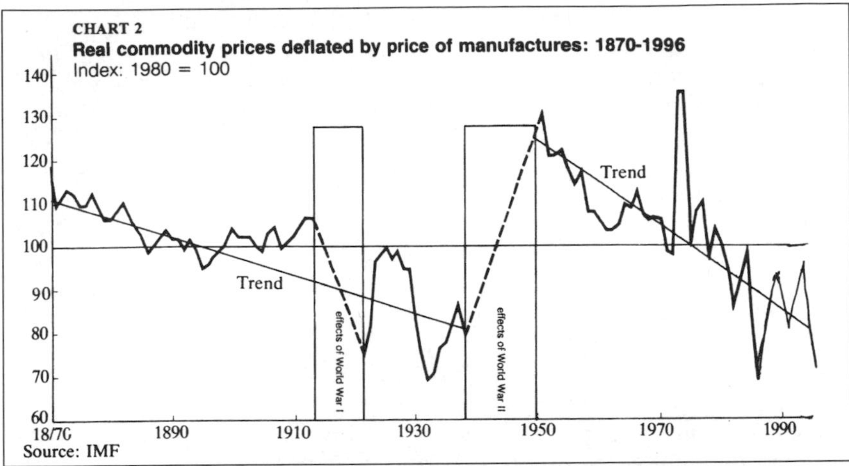

Source: Overseas Development Institute Briefing Paper, March 1998, with extension by Michael Barratt Brown.

companies. An important step towards correcting this abuse would be a requirement of transparency from tax havens like Switzerland and Lichtenstein. The infamous secret accounts in Swiss banks were recently forced open by United States pressure to reveal the gold holdings of holocaust victims. So it can be done.

The greatest assistance that could be provided to these poor countries would be the relaxation of the protection which the rich countries give to their own producers, especially to their agricultural, textiles and electronic industries.

Box 25. First World Protectionism

'... the Third World loses annually about $500 billion dollars from various forms of First World protectionism and market intervention – ten times what they receive annually in foreign assistance.'

UN Development Programme, *Human Development Report 1997*, New York

---

This often spells ruin for Third World farmers who cannot compete with subsidised grain and vegetable oil imports, where the subsidy alone to the First World farmer is many times greater than the price received for the same product grown in the Third World. An end to such protection would not only benefit the people of the Third World but also those of the First World who pay the taxes for financing the subsidies. And it is not mainly the farmers who benefit from these subsidies but the oil companies supplying the fuel, fertiliser, herbicides and pesticides etc. for modern large-scale and ecologically destructive farming.

The International Financial Institutions

The worst aspect of international economic and financial relations we have seen to be the wholly misguided insistence of the World Bank and the IMF as a condition of aid to poor countries on cutting back public expenditures upon which the health and education and social fabric of any country and its development depend. Most recently the Russians were denied assistance unless they persisted with what are called economic reforms. These meant further cuts in public spending, which the Russian Parliament has simply refused to authorise, despite heavy pressure from outside on Mr Yeltsin. The reason for the insistence on cutting public expenditure is that, in the monetarist 'free market' book, there is no other way of ensuring that inflation is controlled and foreign debts are paid, so that capitalists already operating in the country leave their money there and foreign capitalists are attracted to invest there.

There is of course an alternative to monetarism. It consists of policies which were practised under the Bretton Woods Agreement at the end of the Second World War. Financial capital was regulated by international agreement on exchange rates and capital controls. This allowed governments to carry out their own interest rate and tax policies and to sustain full employment and social programmes without the fear of capital flight. Now that the Russian government has chosen to reimpose capital controls, it is said with much lamentation (*Financial Times,* head line, 16.09.98) that Russia is 'harking back to Soviet methods of regulating the foreign exchange market'. These journalists have short memories. Until the 1970s, when President Nixon began to dismantle such foreign exchange market regulation with the support of the British government, it was universally practised.

Returning to practices which obtained during the golden age of high levels of growth of the economy and productivity would not seem to be such a bad idea. It even has the recently won support of the Executive Director of the World Bank, but not of the Managing Director of the IMF (M. Camdessus). It is said by M. Camdessus that today the result of such capital regulation by any government would be the isolation of that country from world sources of capital investment. That also might be no such bad thing, but it has in any case happened already to many of those countries which did liberalise their finances and have seen their economies go from bad to worse. That has of course been the experience of Russia and of most of Sub-Saharan Africa. Liberalisation has for these countries been an unmitigated disaster.

M. Camdessus also argues against those who advocate capital controls as a temporary measure, that temporary measures always become permanent. Depending on the stages of development of their economies almost all countries have moved from protection to freer trade relations. Even the most liberal economists have recognised the case for the protection of infant industries. The World Bank acknowledged that the results of the last round (the so-called Uruguay Round) of negotiations under the General Agreement on Tariffs and Trade, which preceded the creation of the World Trade Organisation, was that the further freeing of trade in goods and services would benefit the rich countries most, and some poor countries would lose out because they would not be able to take advantage of the opportunities made available.

Box 26. Winners and Losers from GATT

'Trade Liberalisation from 2002, based on a 30% cut in tariffs and subsidies, as envisaged in the Uruguay Round is expected to produce net gains of $213 billions. Of this $142 billion (two-thirds) will go to the already industrialised countries with one sixth of the world population. One third of the gains will go to the rest, but all of Africa, Indonesia and the Middle East (apart from the Gulf region) will actually stand to lose – to the extent of $5 billions.

OECD/World Bank, *Trade Liberalisation: Global Economic Implications*, World Bank, 1993

Such unequal distribution of gains would be even truer of the probable results of the secret discussions taking place in the World Trade Organisation for the Multilateral Agreement on Investment (MAI). The secrecy is because there has been such strong opposition from non-

governmental organisations to the leaked proposals, that the big transnational companies have had to conceal their aim of taking away from governments the power to determine their investment decisions and leaving these entirely to the companies. Public opinion in the form of the Jubilee 2000 coalition succeeded in putting debt relief on the agenda of the big industrial powers' meeting in the UK in May 1998, 70,000 people forming a human chain around their meeting place in Birmingham.

There has been a similar response in many countries to MAI, as we recorded earlier, to prevent the even more serious reduction in the ability of governments to make their own decisions about meeting the needs of their people through the control over foreign investment. The alternative being sought by the giant companies of altering the Articles of Agreement setting up the IMF would be even more damaging to national independence. For they are seeking to give to the IMF the actual right to require of any government in exchange for IMF funds that the regulation of capital investment should in effect be denied to elected governments and left to be managed by totally unaccountable corporations.

Transnational corporations are set to become rivals to nation states, many of them, as we have seen, deploying financial resources that greatly exceed the assets and incomes of all but the largest states. Of course, the need for governments to control capital movements into and out of their territories does not rule out the possibility of joint and common action between governments; indeed the multinational nature of the big corporations' activities makes such co-operation essential.

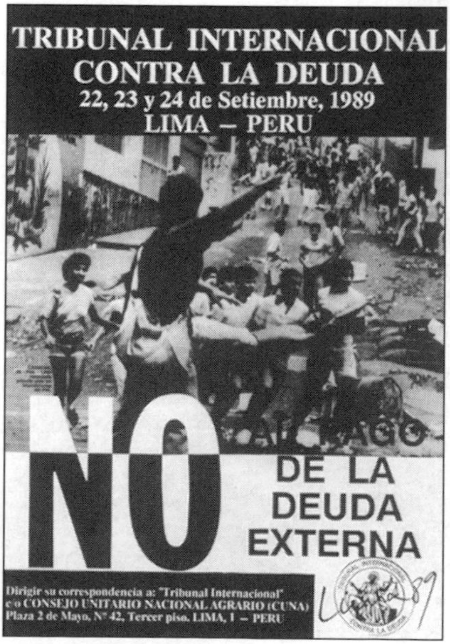

Protests are important, but they need to be backed up by positive proposals. Reform of the IMF and World Bank cannot just be a matter of more transparency, as Mr Blair seems to believe, according to reports of his proposed reforms for the IMF and the World Bank, made in his capacity as 1998 chairman of the G7 (the Group of prime ministers of the seven most industrialised countries). John Eatwell and Lance Taylor, whose criticism of financial liberalisation was quoted earlier, have proposed a new United Nations monitoring organisation to control the two giant financial institutions. This is not at all the same as Mr Blair's proposal for their amalgamation. It could, however be combined with other proposals made in the last few years, and particularly those made on the 50th. anniversary of the 1944 Bretton Woods agreement, under which the IMF and World Bank were founded.

Independent Proposals for Reform

At that time, a consortium of international non-governmental aid agencies (NGOs) ran a campaign proclaiming '50 Years is Enough'. It did not simply propose terminating the lives of the IMF and World Bank at 50, but made important proposals for reform. Since the question of reform of the IMF and the Bank has now been raised by Mr Blair, these NGO proposals of 1994 are worth briefly listing:

- the IDA (International Development Association) which gives soft loans to the poorest countries and the GEF (Global Environment Facility) should both be legally and financially separated from the World Bank;
- the IMF should be restricted to technical assistance on monetary and financial policies and mobilising capital and debt relief with adequate funds supplied by the governments of the richer countries;
- the Bank should reduce its large scale infrastructure projects to 10% of its loan portfolio and expand support for broad-based sustainable food production;
- both the Bank and the IMF should pursue a more open information policy;
- the inspection panel, established as a result of outside pressure, should be expanded to include independent, non-Bank appointees.

Beyond these points, it is essential that the independent advisory bodies, stipulated in the Articles of Agreement of the Bank and the IMF, which have never been made operational, should be instituted:

- A Fund (IMF)Council
- A Bank Advisory Council, with wide representation
- Each loan committee of the Bank 'to include an expert selected by the Governor representing the member in whose territory the project is located.'

It must seem incredible that such minimal forms of accountability were simply overridden. But none of this would bring us back to the international financial structure which Keynes envisaged in negotiating at Bretton Woods on behalf of the British government and which Mr George Soros has been reviving.

Keynes's original proposals which were vetoed by the United States would have given to an independent international bank, not subject to US supervision, the power of international currency creation and of lender of last resort and the resources to finance the growth of world trade without reliance on gold or the US dollar. Special consideration was to be given to guaranteeing that the value of the commodities of the ex-colonial countries would be recognised as an alternative form of security to holdings of gold or dollars.

There is no going back to the circumstances in which Keynes was making his proposals in the middle of World War Two, when popular support for the war effort was of crucial importance and the popular appeal of the Soviet armies' victories over the Nazis was at its most powerful, both considerations forcing the leaders of the main capitalist countries to embrace quite radical political and economic policies. There are no such forces at work today *pace* Mr Soros. On the other hand, the hegemonic position of the United States, which was so total in 1944, has been somewhat eroded. Keynes was working on the assumption that world power would be shared in the future, as in the UN Security Council – between the USA, UK, France, the USSR and China and, no doubt after their defeat, Germany and Japan.

That position of great power equality is much more nearly what obtains today, despite the overwhelming military power of the USA. Europe, moreover, is moving towards Economic and Monetary Union, which not only presents a major challenge to the United States, but indicates the possibility of some common actions entrusting to genuinely international civil servants the management of international finances with a new aim, that of restoring full employment.

Setting Criteria for the Bankers

Such trust would be dependent on the civil servants being assigned criteria for their operations, such as to comprise employment and environmental measures along with the control of inflation. There are widely felt fears that we have already noted that German and other bankers managing European Central Bank policies will be unduly restrictive with inflation control as their only criterion, just like the Bank of England under the Blair-Brown regime.

Bankers seem to have forgotten that the actual objectives laid down for the European System of Central Banks (ESCB) are two fold, not only price stability but 'without prejudice to the objective of price stability the ESCB shall support the general economic policies of the Community with a view to contributing to the achievement of the objectives of the Community, as laid down in Article 2.' And Article 2 specifies the task of the Community

> 'to promote throughout the Community a harmonious and balanced development of economic activities, sustainable and non-inflationary growth respecting the environment, a high degree of convergence of economic performance, a high level of employment and of social protection, the raising of the standard of living and the quality of life, and economic and social

cohesion and solidarity among Member States.'

This wording is remarkably similar to that used at the founding of the WTO. The commitment not just to 'a high level of employment' but to 'full employment' and to sustainable development may be regarded by some as mere rhetorical flourishes to soften up critical Third World peoples. But the words can be used in argument against actions that fail to make them real and as a basis for alternative policies to those actually being pursued by the existing financial institutions. How realistic are such policies?

Box 27. Commitment of the Parties to the Founding of the WTO

'agreed that their relations in the field of trade and economic endeavour should be conducted with a view to raising standards of living, ensuring full employment and a large and steadily growing volume of real income and effective demand and expanding the production and trade in goods and services, while allowing for the optimal use of the world's resources in accordance with the objective of sustainable development, seeking both to protect and preserve the environment and enhance the means for doing so in a manner consistent with their respective needs and concerns at different levels of economic development.'

GATT, *Final Act Embodying the Results of the Uruguay Round of Multilateral Trade Negotiations*, 15 December, 1993

CHAPTER 8

Long-term Change – within Capitalism

Alternative policies will have to go beyond the remedies we have been looking at so far for staving off the gathering world crisis. **For these remedies have been essentially palliatives, nonetheless important for alleviating the sufferings of the unemployed in the First World and of the starving in the Third, but they do nothing to prevent the persistent tendency to polarisation within the system.** They are like Ptolemy's epicycles designed to correct the errors of calculations based on the assumption that the sun revolved around the earth. More epicycles had always to be added. So it is with the corrections required in the interests of human welfare in an economy based on the assumption that return to capital is central, and not human needs.

The socialist answer to capitalist inequalities and crises has always been to replace the market by conscious planning, not for all purposes but for the allocation of resources, so as to ensure that the needs of the people are met.

This answer has been largely discredited because of the economic failures of the Soviet and East European planning systems. The failures cannot be denied, but that they had any connection with democratic socialism can be denied. There was no democracy; and the Soviet leaders engaged in the arms race with the United States without consultation with their people and at the expense of deteriorating living standards for all but a small elite. It is of course this elite which has inherited the privatised enterprises of the former Soviet economy.

The arms race has to be understood as the precipitate disaster for the Soviet Union, engineered by the United States to preempt resources for military expenditure which the Soviet Union could ill afford, but which the United States could not only afford but could use to maintain its economic growth.

We have noted, however, that, while the years between 1979 and 1990 were years of most rapid growth in the USA, the average earnings of American workers during this period did not grow. For workers in the Soviet

Union the experience was actually negative, and starting from a much lower level. The military industrial complex absorbed everything, and, in the race to win, the waste of resources was seriously debilitating in an economy that after the devastation of two World Wars started at a very low level.

Soviet planning systems were no more than bureaucratic controls imposed upon the people, in the pursuit of world military superiority, through decisions in which they had not participated, but accepted because the system gave a guaranteed wage and some degree of economic and social security for all, albeit at a low level. The loss of even this basic security has been a disaster for millions of Russians and is what makes many of them hanker after the old days of the Soviet economy. It is a matter of some importance in relation to the comments of foreign journalists about Russia's revival of 'Soviet state controls' that Russia's proposed state controls today are subject to the decisions of a Parliament that has shown itself to be quite exceptionally independent of the executive. But the crucial point is that Russia and the rest of the old Soviet Union have to be regarded as Third World countries with the same problems as many others – of foreign debt and inadequate protection against foreign capitalist exploitation.

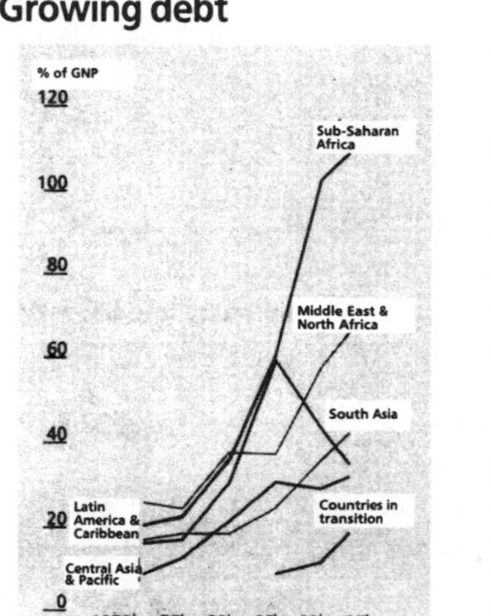

In the period 1971-1993, the total external debt expressed as a proportion of GNP, increased in every region of the world. The high levels of Latin American debt in the 1980s have decreased since then. The sub-Saharan African debt continues to grow and has already surpassed the region's GNP.

Source: World Bank, World Debt Tables 1994-95, vol. 2, Washington DC, 1994.
Note: In the Sub-Saharan Africa data, South Africa is not included.

International Economic Cooperation

How then could we move beyond the reduction of the poor countries' debts to tackle the whole gamut of unequal relations between the industrialised countries and the poorer countries of the Third World? We have already noted the abuse of transfer pricing by transnational companies and the need to correct this abuse by a requirement of transparency from tax havens like Switzerland and Lichtenstein. The free trade system can also be challenged, not by increasing measures of protection, but by reducing those maintained by the rich countries.

In the words of an Indian delegate to an early meeting of the General

Agreement on Tariffs and Trade (the GATT), free trade is in effect a one-way street, down which the rich countries can move with their goods and services, but with no chance for the poor to move up.

The greatest assistance that could be made to these poor countries would be the relaxation of the protection which the rich countries give to their own producers, especially to their agricultural, textiles and electronic industries. We have already noted how, far from practising themselves what they preach about free trade, the rich are the worst protectionists. Reducing the barriers they have erected to protect themselves would mean taking on some of the most entrenched vested interests in the United States. How would this be done? What bargain could be made to strengthen the position of the less developed countries?

The first task is to undermine totally the commitment of the international financial institutions and the bankers everywhere to monetarist dogma, which is used as a cover for giving a free rein to those with most money.

The worst aspect of international economic and financial relations we have seen to be the wholly misguided insistence of the World Bank and the IMF as a condition of aid on cutting back public expenditures in the less developed countries, upon which the health and education and social fabric of any country depends. Most recently the Russians were denied assistance unless they persisted with what are called economic reforms. These meant further cuts in public spending, which the Russian Parliament simply refused to authorise, despite heavy pressure from outside on Mr Yeltsin.

Box 28. Inflation or Starvation

'Starvation induced by mass unemployment is much worse. What led to Nazism in Germany was not the hyperinflation of 1923-24 but the mass unemployment of the 1930s. Forcing Russia into starvation by insisting that it balances its budget, or shore up the exchange rate of the rouble, so that the Western banks can pay their shareholders and not suffer for their misjudgements as they deserve to, would be playing with much worse than fire.'

Meghnad Desai, 'Russia must put bread before theory', *The Guardian*, 21.9.98

The reason for the insistence on cutting public expenditure is that, in the monetarist 'free market' book, there is no other way of ensuring that inflation is controlled and foreign debts are paid, so that capitalists already operating in the country leave their money there and foreign capitalists are attracted to invest there. But this is only true of extreme cases, where governments are not raising taxes to meet their expenditure and where governments can exercise no controls over capital movements – the Russian case. And some countries have survived for many years without foreign investment, as the Soviet Union did.

The Bretton Woods Alternative

It is said that there is no alternative to current IMF policies, but there is indeed an alternative. It was practised under the Bretton Woods Agreement in the first years after the end of the Second World War. Financial capital was regulated by international agreement on exchange rates and on the limits of capital export controls. This allowed governments to carry out their own interest rate and tax policies within these parameters and to sustain full employment and social programmes, including income redistribution from rich to poor, without the fear of capital flight. Returning to practices which obtained during the golden age of high levels of growth of the economy and productivity would not seem to be such a bad idea, but what would it involve today?

The answer is nothing less than a major challenge to the whole current system. While official opinion is swinging back, even in the IMF and the World Bank, to the need for temporary capital controls by defaulting states, the idea of regulating free markets is fundamentally self-contradictory. What is needed is international government management of interest rates and exchanges within the framework of a common world money. Yet, this is still regarded as just 'loony'. Its time will come, just as the time of the euro has arrived.

It has been difficult enough to persuade most businesses and informed persons that these things can be managed in Europe under a common economic policy. How much more difficult would it be to move to a higher level of world-wide management, where there are far greater differences of income and living standards? Yet, the introduction of a common framework of European institutions has begun to bring people, and especially young people, together to talk the same language and to delight in common sports and song and other cultural contests. A common coinage can only advance such unity. But there are some people making their living from the world's currency exchanges and from speculating in them, and they derive their power from the general belief in the efficacy of markets.

There is no doubt that a united

European Economic and Monetary Union (EMU) could have a powerful influence in correcting United States domination of the world economy, but it could also begin the process of challenging the role of the market and thus the power of the global companies. This would imply placing socialist objectives ahead of capitalist objectives, as M. Jospin in France and Herr Schroeder in Germany have committed themselves to do, and disengaging New Labour from the United States embrace. It would mean putting full employment and the elimination of poverty at the top of the political agenda everywhere.

Global conferences in the 1990s of the United Nations agencies, not only the UNDP, but the World Health Organisation, the UN International Children's Emergency Fund (UNICEF), the UN Educational, Scientific and Cultural Organisation (UNESCO), the UN Population Fund (UNFPA) have all committed themselves to a common programme of poverty eradication. The measures required are now well understood and have been carefully costed. The cost amounts to less than 5% of the wealth of a few billionaires. These UN agencies still need the political will for action to follow up on their recommendations. And there may be the need to create new institutions dedicated to world-wide full employment and environmental protection.

The Tobin Tax on speculators can be put to work not only for debt redemption but for measures of poverty eradication.

The New Information Technology

Much hope can now be placed on the effect of the new information technology. Despite the secrecy surrounding the decisions of the financial institutions and the big corporations, far more people are informed of what is happening in the world economy, and informed far more quickly, than ever before. Electronic communication, moreover, is creating wholly new forms of economic relations, with lower capital-labour ratios, which can serve to weaken the power of the capital of the giant transnational companies. Micro-technology also reduces the demand for many essential raw materials. This is not good news for raw material producers in the Third World, but food producers should survive, if subsidies for Northern agriculture can be cut back.

There is no doubt that many jobs will be destroyed by the new technology. An estimate made in Texas suggests that in order to produce 3 million new jobs there by 2020, it will be necessary to create 15 million and lose 12 million. Donald Hicks of the University of Texas argues that **the task of the state and the trade unions should never be to protect jobs but to create them.**

The most exciting aspect of the new information technology is the freedom it gives to the individual. But individuals will find themselves isolated and powerless without a strong framework of social and community organisation,

Who is going to buy the goods?

and of state support.

The greatest danger is that communities will fail to make use of the opportunities provided by the new technology, before the giant companies like Murdoch's empire freeze up access by imposing their own exclusive equipment and standards. The new information technology is not just about computers – 200 million of them today, 500 million by 2002. The old joke about 'chips with everything' has come true. There may be 200 million computers, but there are 6 billion chips at work outside computers – in your car, in your plastic card, under your dog's skin, in every new hotel door 'key' (see graph on page xiii). In the most complicated uses, aeroplanes can now 'talk' to each other and can probably land more safely than with human air traffic controllers.

The problem will be to support the finding of new jobs and the transition to them. Everything we have seen in this book tells us that this will not happen just because we help to make people more employable. Governments will have to be constantly helping to create new jobs, not only directly but through their encouragement of and support for non-governmental and community organisations. There have been many indications of such a development, although recent cuts in public spending have held them back.

Shorter Working Time

The easiest way to find new jobs is to reduce working time. Jacques Delors in his 1996 paper on 'Development: A New Model', prepared for the European Socialists, which we quoted earlier, provides some interesting figures. In the 1920s the average European man spent 100,000 hours at work in his life-time, that is over a 50 year span some 2000 hours a year. Today he spends only 70,000 at work and in 25 years time it may be only 40,000. That might be 1000 hours a year over 40 years. Yet in the last few years, those in work have been working longer hours than before, some working 70 hours a week, perhaps as much as 3500 a year, while others have no work. Inquiries made in several European countries including the UK reveal that much overtime is in effect compulsory (it is in the contract or in some other way part of the job), and many workers would prefer to work shorter hours, some even if their pay was correspondingly reduced.

Workers in the UK have the longest hours in Europe, over a fifth of all men and women doing over 48 hours. For 48 weeks a year 48 hours a week adds up to 2300 annual hours. The best practice in Europe is represented by Germany, where the average is 1500 annual working hours. Elsewhere in Europe the average is some 1700 hours. In the USA it is 1800 and in Japan at least 2200. The aim of European Socialists has been to reduce the average to a 1000 hour year, with an immediate target of 1400 hours a year.

Box 29. The Thousand Hour Year

'The Cohesion Report estimates that a progressive approach to such a policy [of reducing working hours], with an annual reduction of less than half of one per cent a year, could create up to 10 million new jobs in the Union by 2002, or a level equivalent to two thirds of registered unemployment in 1992.'

Stuart Holland, *Economic and Social Cohesion in the 1990s*, Report to DGs. II, V, VI, and XVI of the Commission of the European Communities, Brussels, November, 1992

It is assumed that a reduction in working hours generates a spontaneous increase in labour productivity, not of course equal to the actual reduction, but possibly to half that amount. This is the result of rationalisation in the workplace, reduction in absences from sickness, less work accidents due to fatigue and other similar improvements in worker morale.

The calculation of working hours is made by the proposers of shorter working time always in terms of a major shortening of the working year. This is because there is widespread interest in flexibility, not just by employers who want reduced restrictions on the length and frequency of working time, but by workers too who want greater control over their own time. This comprises the desire for part-time work by women, and men also, with young children. In the ten years from 1983 to 1992, 60% of the new jobs created in Britain were part time and since then the proportion has been even higher. And this situation obtained also in France, The Netherlands and Ireland. Of course many men would have preferred a full-time job, but most women would not.

Part-time employment is sought not only by women, however, but by those with an involvement in voluntary activities; and one of the great advantages of reduced working time for many people is the freedom to engage in unpaid and informal work. Flexibility is also sought by many who look for periods of training and education and for preparation for retirement and for sabbaticals to pursue interests other than their regular work. We have earlier noted that the pace of change in the new technology makes this almost essential. Already in Denmark, 5% of the work force is at any one time on training leave, parental leave or sabbatical leave.

The concept of lifelong learning has been taken up by governments in several countries, most recently by New Labour in Britain. The aim is partly to overcome the inequalities of educational provision in the past, but partly to allow men and most especially women to adjust to the changes in the economy and in working life brought about by technological advances and the consequent requirement of new and updated skills. For this to be more than a privilege of the already well educated and highly skilled, it will be necessary for workers through their unions to win from their employers the concession of paid educational leave. And for women to have equal opportunities, there will need to be an extension of provision for paternity leave and a massive increase in child care facilities.

All the facilities involved in providing for a fuller and more flexible life than the traditional three ages – of education, work and retirement – will in themselves demand a great expansion of employment in the educational and caring services, whether paid or voluntary. But, more than this, the application of the new information technology increasingly requires combinations of skills in one person that were previously divided between several. Already, the TUC has reported that there are over a million workers who hold two jobs. This may be because they need them both to make ends meet, but there is much evidence that it is because they have scarce skills which are in strong demand.

The danger exists of a new kind of inequality emerging between those who have the necessary wide range of skills and those who have none. To take one example, which Jacques Delors takes in his paper to the European Socialists, the work of secretaries can be upgraded or downgraded by the advent of information technnology. Tele-working is another example where the application of electronic technology does not at all necessarily end the oppression of boring, repetitive work, as in the printing out of air tickets by Indian women workers.

A Network Economy

The economy of the future will be a 'network economy', producers and consumers being connected together increasingly by direct communication

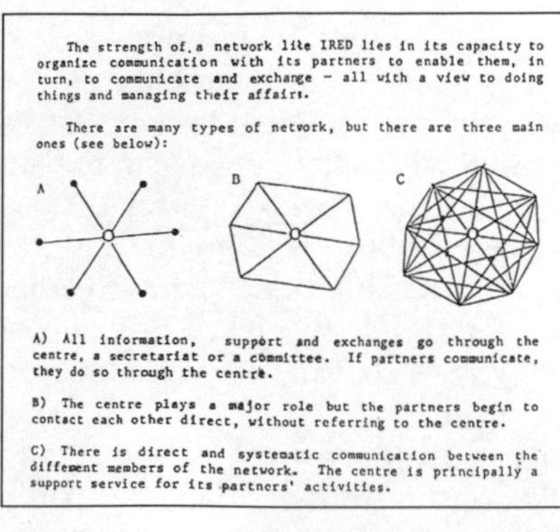

The strength of a network like IRED lies in its capacity to organize communication with its partners to enable them, in turn, to communicate and exchange – all with a view to doing things and managing their affairs.

There are many types of network, but there are three main ones (see below):

A B C

A) All information, support and exchanges go through the centre, a secretariat or a committee. If partners communicate, they do so through the centre.

B) The centre plays a major role but the partners begin to contact each other direct, without referring to the centre.

C) There is direct and systematic communication between the different members of the network. The centre is principally a support service for its partners' activities.

without the present chains of intermediaries. This must greatly reduce the need for credit and the importance of finance, although 'just in time' systems seem at present greatly to lengthen the period of waiting for consumers to obtain delivery. This network economy involves not just the use of the 'internet' for your library, your shopping, your entertainment; it is the development of a new way of relating to each other in all our economic activities and a new way of measuring economic growth.

The old way was to measure output in terms of labour input, which as labour was saved gave us so-called higher productivity. But much of the output was wasted or of little use or actually needed to make good the negative results in pollution and environmental destruction of other output. In future the output of robots may be measured in the old way, and measures of natural resource saving and environmental protection already exist, waiting only to be applied. The use of human resources, however, will need new measures, the result of human deliberation and choice on a democratic basis, not the result of price movements in markets dominated by a few giant transnational companies.

Buying and selling in the market will continue but it will not determine the allocation of resources. Nor will some centralised bureaucracy. Networking implies cooperation with others as equals, not in hierarchies of command and control. The economy of trust has to displace the orders down the line. Already, there are successful examples of networks of suppliers and consumers – in the fair trade business for example and in LETS, the Local Exchange and Trading Systems, which are based on trust and participation. While markets will still be used, they will increasingly be subordinated to

common human decision on resource allocation. Goods will still appear on the supermarket shelves, not only in reality but on your computer shopping screen and, more and more they will be chosen because they appeal directly from the producer to the consumer, as *café direct* does for example.

Box 30. A Network Economy

'As networks have permeated our world, the economy has come to resemble an ecology of organisms, interlinked and co-evolving, constantly in flux, deeply tangled, ever expanding at its edges. As we know from recent biological studies, no balance exists in nature; rather as evolution proceeds, there is perpetual disruption as new species displace old, as natural biomes shift in their make-up, and as organisms and environments transform each other.'

Kevin Kelly, 'New Rules for the New Economy', *Wired*, September 1997

Such a revolution in the economy does not by any means imply the ending of the inequalities that disfigure and destabilise the current system. Many of the proposals for immediate action set forth in previous chapters could still be adopted, but they will need a new framework to end the polarisation of wealth and poverty which is causing the breakdown of the old capitalist framework. Mr Blair says that he has found it and it is a third way between capitalism and socialism. We need to examine this before considering what might follow after capitalism.

Workers' demonstration, General Strike, 1926.

CHAPTER 9

A "Third Way" or a Different Way?

It has been proposed that what we need is a 'third way' between the two old ways of commands and of markets, a way that is supposed to contain a bit of both as a mixed economy. This is an old idea that has recently been revived by Mr Blair and his new guru, Professor Anthony Giddens of the London School of Economics. In his book, *The Third Way*, Giddens states that 'There was a time when a lot of us thought there was an alternative to capitalism, called socialism. That's no longer an alternative, at least at the moment.' His reasons are based first on the experience of the East European command economies, secondly on the neglect of ecological issues and of the importance of the family, but fourthly on the changing class structure of our society.

The command economies never were any sort of democratic socialism and, if they had been at all democratic, the environment, which most affects poor people, might not have been so neglected. Undoubtedly the whole concept of the family has changed, but to make it less rather than more central to our lives. The average size of households in Britain has fallen from 3.1 to 2.4 in thirty years. The issue of class structure raised by Giddens is probably the most important.

What Has Changed?

Socialism, as Giddens correctly observes, arose from the struggles of a working class of wage labourers dispossessed from the land, dependent for work upon owners of capital and largely excluded from political power. Such a working class with its class consciousness, he maintains, however, is dwindling and gradually being outnumbered by a diverse middle class of white collar employees; and these 'tend to work in decentralised, non-hierarchical work settings.' This is the basis of the Blair Project.

It may be true that increasing numbers of people feel that they are not 'working class' and are either middle class or classless, but objectively the fact is that, as Giddens concedes, they are still mainly *employees*, and subject to just as great, if not greater, insecurity and exploitation in their employment as ever. The self-employed, who are for the most part less, rather than more, secure in their employment, increased rapidly during the 1980s, but still only number about 3 million out of a workforce of 27 million in Britain today; and their number is now declining. Of those who are employed, manual occupations make up a half of the male total and manual and clerical nearly two thirds of the female total. Taking into account the unemployed and the manual work of most of the self employed, two thirds of the population must still be thought of as manual workers.

The question of work settings has not received adequate analysis. On the one hand, the average size of establishments, both factories and offices, has greatly diminished, so that there are no longer so many large units, with massed work forces. The proportion of workers in Britain in manufacturing units of more than 1000 employees has fallen from 36% of the total to 14% in the last 35 years and the proportion in units of less than 50 has risen from 11% to 27%. The great reduction in total manufacturing employment, where large numbers of workers were concentrated, has of course greatly affected the overall picture of decentralisation. So has the reduction almost to nothing of employment in mining and shipbuilding.

Work in offices has not proved to be any more liberating than factory work. Average hours worked have actually increased over the last few decades with, as we have seen, long hours of involuntary overtime. Industrial accidents have increased. Stress at work is widely reported and the evidence of less hierarchical work settings is limited to the higher ranks and to certain more advanced industries.

Giddens explains militancy among nurses and other health workers, teachers and bank staff in terms of what he calls the 'Balkanisation in promotion where you get to a certain level and then are stuck.' That sounds rather hierarchical; and these groups of workers account for nearly half the workforce and much more than half of those organised in unions. Not all the militancy is associated with claims for pay to be kept in line with private industry. Much of it is concerned precisely with complaints about working conditions, redundancies and dismissals.

There is increasing pressure from management for performance related pay, performance to be determined by the employer, and this is now being extended under New Labour leadership from the Health Service to education. The huge increase in the number of part-time women employees, with little or no statutory rights or trade union protection, has greatly increased the numbers and degree of exploitation in the retailing and non-professional services. A minimum wage set very low hardly helps.

A workers' charter, not just a social chapter, must be the aim of organised workers if they are to raise their status.

Professor Giddens says that he feels 'it is a great mistake to see politics centring solely around the issue of inequality. There are so many other

More taxes?

issues, including most centrally of all, how to respond to a globalised society.' We have seen that the central issue of globalisation is also the growing inequalities – this time between states and regions as well as between classes. We quoted earlier the facts of an actual deterioration of living standards over two decades not only in Africa and the Middle East but among wage earners in the United States itself.

Box 31. New Labour's Third Way – 'humanised capitalism'

'New Labour has a middle class constituency, potentially a radical Centre, which can be reached, and won over by Third Way policies that stress decency and civic virtue...It has to apply to corporations, to the wealthy. It must be a principle running through the whole of society. The key thing about the Third Way is how do you produce a sort of humanised capitalism, because at the minute no one can see beyond that...You have to re-educate people about paying taxes, that it is to some extent a civic obligation, not just a burden ... To actually reintegrate the more affluent in society, you've got to use a range of devices, including building a model of a more benign nationalism.'

Anthony Giddens, interview with Mike Naughton, *Tribune*, 2.10.98
Based on Giddens' book, *The Third Way*, Polity Press, 1998

A Fourth Way – 'Humanised' Socialism?

Humanising capitalism is unfortunately for Professor Giddens and Mr Blair a contradiction in terms. The aim and driving force of capitalism is the accumulation of capital from the exploitation of labour. Our common humanity attests to the fact that all men and women are ends in themselves and cannot properly be employed as means to another's ends. Mr Blair makes much of this in talking frequently about the 'equal worth of each individual'. Yet, in the work which most of us do to earn a living – in office, factory, shop, mine, construction site, transport system or communications – we have to perform tasks that are set by others, to realise goals that have been determined by still others, often primarily for their gain. We are being used as means and not ends. The system requires this, subject only to some necessary consultation.

What then would be the result should any employer say that he (it is very rarely she) will pay to his workers' a wage equal to the full value of the work they do – as men and women of equal worth – in contributing on a voluntary basis to the final goods or services for sale, with deductions only for agreed overhead costs to maintain the business and keep up with future developments? He would be unable to raise any outside capital because he would not be making a profit for those who supply the capital. He would only be able to borrow against his own assets; no bank or private financier would take the risk of possible loss, without security guarantees. In a competitive market he would almost certainly go bust.

Then, it may be said, that the profit is a payment for taking a risk, in conditions where there may be no profit but only loss. Of course this is true in certain projects especially among small and medium sized enterprises. But it is simply not true for the giant multinationals, whose profits are guaranteed – unless they make grave errors of judgement – by the monopoly positions which they occupy. And it is typical of the small and medium sized enterprises that it is men and women with hardly any capital who take great risks with their own money and have to pay most of the profit they earn to banks and others who lend them funds for their projects without taking any risk at all. If it is hard to imagine 'humanising capitalism', what about socialism?

What was called socialism in the Soviet Union and in Eastern Europe and what went for socialism in the UK and other parts of Western Europe lacked the necessary element of democratic control over political *and* economic decisions to ensure that every individual was treated as being of equal worth. Of course no one supposed that the contribution of each would be equal, but the right of each to a say in how his or her work was organised and how and what payments were made would be essential to such treatment.

Box 32. Socialist Self-management

...'self-management' as 'the most important means of strengthening the feeling of common ownership, so that the workers themselves feel that they are in charge of the socialist property allotted to the collective, something that is theirs and not someone else's.'

Abel Aganbegyan, *The Challenge: The Economics of Perestroika*, Hutchinson, 1988

Democratic Planning

The answer of socialists to the anarchy of capitalism and its tendency to generate inequalities and end up from time to time in unstable conditions and ultimate slump has always been the plan. Instead of resources being allocated according to the uncertain results of competition in the market, they would be allocated according to an agreed plan, designed in theory to meet the needs of the people. In the Soviet Union and Eastern Europe the needs that were met were those of a small bureaucratic elite. But this was the result of the low level of political and economic development of the peoples of the Soviet Union.

There was no inherent reason in a planned economy why the plan should not have been subject to democratic controls at all levels. Instead of being centralised, economic decision-making could have been decentralised, without losing the advantages of planned allocation of resources. That this did not happen in the Soviet Union was partly the result of the personality of Stalin, but even more the result of being a state under siege and having responded from the start by constructing a war economy.

Before the advent of the new information technology, the possibility anywhere even in conditions of peace of obtaining wide participation in planning decisions was not good. Now this has changed. On the one hand, information can become immediately and widely available as soon as it is loaded onto the Internet. The Starr Report on President Clinton's affair with Monica Lewinsky was seen by millions of people all over the world at the same time that members of the United States Congress could see it.

On the other hand, the Internet is becoming used increasingly for shopping, with the possibility of ordering direct from items shown up on the screen, as if one was picking them up from the shelves. The extension of this possibility to voting for particular local and national policies presented in speeches and resolutions could involve a whole population in a new form of direct democracy. Conferences can be held with people participating from many parts of the world through electronic communication.

It is worth summarising the argument of Paul Cockshott and Allin Cottrell because it indicates the possibility of combining planning and the market in a quite new way, which brings the preferences of consumers directly into the planning process through computerised information and thus eliminates the top-downward nature of planning. Cottrell is an economist and Cockshott is a university lecturer in computer science and they have no doubt that such information can be collected, stored and utilised for planning purposes.

Table 1. *Macroeconomic accounting relationships*

Generation of savings	
Household:	$S_h = W + J_b + J_g + \xi_h - C_h - T_h - Z_h$
Business:	$S_b = \Pi - J_b - T_b - Z_b - eZ_b^*$
Government:	$S_g = T_h + T_b - C_g - J_g - Z_g - eZ_g^*$
Financial system:	$0 = Z_h + Z_b + Z_g - \xi_h$
Foreign:	$S_f = e[M + Z_b^* + Z_g^* - E]$
Resource balance	
	$S_h + S_b + S_g + S_f = W + \Pi - (C_h + C_g) + e(M - E)$
Investment–saving balance	
	$(I_h - S_h) + (I_b - S_b) + (I_g - S_g) = S_f$
Accumulation	
Household:	$(I_h - S_h) = \Delta D_h - \Delta H_h$
Business:	$(I_b - S_b) = \Delta D_b + e\Delta D_b^*$
Government:	$(I_g - S_g) = \Delta D_g + e\Delta D_g^*$
Financial system:	$0 = \Delta H_h - (\Delta D_h + \Delta D_b + \Delta D_g) - e\Delta R^*$
Foreign:	$0 = S_f - e(\Delta D_b^* + \Delta D_g^*) + e\Delta R^*$
Spreads	
Interest rate:	$\Sigma_i = i - [i^* + (\Delta e / e)^E] = i - (i^* + \hat{e}^E)$
Capital gains:	$\Sigma_Q = (\Delta Q / Q)^E - [i^* + (\Delta e / e)^E = \hat{Q}^E - (i^* + \hat{e}^E)$

Box 33. Planning and Information

'We are proposing a system of computerised planning which involves the simulation of the behaviour of the economy in great detail. To make this feasible the central computers must be supplied with copious amounts of technical information, for instance lists of the products being produced and regular updates on the technology used in each production process. Other computer systems will have to record the available stocks of each type of raw material and every model of machine so that these constraints can be fed into the system.'

W. Paul Cockshott & Allin Cottrell, *Towards a New Socialism*, Spokesman, 1993

But we must notice that these experts make it clear that much of the information needed is at present held in secret by the big companies and accessible only to them. Cockshott and Cottrell also recognise very clearly that planning is not just a technical problem, but a social one. It is a matter of involving people, and at all levels.

For planning to be democratised, the necessary social measures and incentives must be in place, so that people are motivated to supply accurate information and to use it for the public good and not for private gain. It was the lack of any such motivation that made Soviet planning grossly inefficient and unjust. But managers in a capitalist economy are equally likely to overestimate their current input requirements and exaggerate the benefits of their particular projects, unless they are kept in check by the forces of competition. In a planned economy the computer simulation of all economic activity, given open and correct information, can take the place of competition.

A central element in the Cockshott and Cottrell vision is the marking of all consumer goods, in addition to a market price, with their labour values, that is the total amount of social labour required, both directly and indirectly, to produce them. This can be calculated from computerised information, and can then be compared by shoppers with the market price, which depends on supply and demand. It is assumed that everybody knows the labour value of their own work. If the price of a good is above its labour value, this means that people are prepared to work more hours than the labour time required to produce that good in order to obtain it. Contrariwise, if people do not 'value' a good at its full labour content, then it is clear to all including the planners that labour devoted to its production is of below average effectiveness. Cockshott and Cottrell call this valuation the 'marketing algorithm'.

Resources can then be allocated by the planners, not according to market profits, which may be the result of monopoly positions and secret transfer pricing, but according to the consumer goods, marketing algorithm.

To secure for the workers by hand or by brain the full fruits of their industry and the most equitable distribution thereof that may be possible upon the basis of the common ownership of the means of production, distribution and exchange, and the best obtainable system of popular administration and control of each industry or service.
Labour Party Constitution Clause IV (4)

Signature

The Labour Party 150 Walworth Road London SE17 1JT. 071-701 1234.

Enterprises showing an especially effective use of social labour will be assigned additional resources including labour. Those showing persistent below-average effectiveness will have to revise their methods or lose labour to other uses. Such an economy would not guarantee workers a job in any particular enterprise, but they could be guaranteed employment, because resources would be moved in line with the marketing algorithm.

Social Ownership

There remains the vexed question of property relations. Who is to own what? The private ownership of capital determines the working of the capitalist system. It ensures some competition and some motivation to be efficient – for the managers a share in the profits, for the workers sometimes a similar carrot, but more generally the stick of unemployment. Socialism assumes social ownership, but not at all necessarily of everything. Labour's old constitution Clause 4 did not say: public ownership of everything, but only as the necessary *basis* for workers to receive the full value of their product.

The right not to be exploited is a right, along with the right to work and to education and a healthy environment. These are citizen rights respecting the equal worth of all, and cannot be qualified by specifying corresponding obligations, as Mr Blair and his guru Professor Giddens propose. They follow from a previous condition of deprivation. Of course, citizenship does involve obligations as well as rights, but not as a specific *quid pro quo.*

Social ownership can take many forms and should rightly do so. Large scale undertakings of the sort of the old nationalised industries are by no means the preferred form, although the result today of the breaking up of the electricity industry and of the railways has shown that they had some merits; and the need for an overall energy policy becomes more obvious with every coal pit that is closed for ever. Social ownership was envisaged by Sidney Webb, who wrote Clause 4, as including a wide range of cooperatives and municipal undertakings as well as state owned enterprises.

The more decentralised the ownership, the more possible becomes the full participation of workers and consumers in management and delivery.

LEVELS AND AVERAGE POPULATION	RESPONSIBILITIES	RESOURCES
Wards/ parishes 2,500	Small workshops. Land and housing. Gardens and small parks. Recreational facilities. Home helps, nurses and crèches.	Own produce and rents *plus* grants from districts
Districts 50,000	Shops, hotels, restaurants. Smaller factories and offices. Streets, sewers, parks. Libraries, galleries, theatres, radio. Education to fifteen and adult. Clinics and doctors. Local employment centres.	Own income from production *plus* grants from centre
Counties 1,000,000	Larger factories and farms. Planning, roads (except trunk) Hospitals, fire service Universities, polytechnics, technical colleges. Local courts and police	Own income from production and services *plus* grants from centre
Regions 6,000,000	Major factories (high technology). Regional banks. Institutes of science, medicine, culture, TV Power supplies, ports, rivers, water, forests.	Own income from production, subject to national taxation
Nation 10 to 30,000,000	National enterprises (in steel, heavy engineering and chemicals). Parliament and committees. National planning. Posts and telephones. Railways and trunk roads. National courts. National institutes	Own income from production and taxation, from which grants payable to lower levels
Federation 400,000,000	Federal enterprises (air, sea, energy). Parliament and committees. Federal planning. Currency and banking. Defence and foreign policy. International transport. Federal courts.	Income from own enterprises, taxation and borrowing

International links. On the basis, not of international planning, but of international agreements, supervised by United Nations agencies for planned exchanges.

Figure 13. Model of a decentralized economy with social ownership and democratic control of executive responsibilities

I have suggested elsewhere the establishment of several levels of ownership of resources for producing goods and services, right down to the parish or ward, with some element of overlap and competition and room for the special interests of consumers through non-governmental organisations. ('Models for Building a New Social Order' in *Models in Political Economy*, Penguin, 1995).

With such decentralisation of ownership and management, the work of the planning authorities would be concerned with the overall allocation of resources and particularly with resource conservation and the protection of the environment. In the capitalist market and in the wholly undemocratic Soviet planning system, there has been no incentive to save resources or prevent pollution if production costs could thereby be made more competitive. Government regulation has proved largely ineffective and has in many countries been recently relaxed to attract investors looking for reduced direct production costs.

The costs to the environment, for example, have been external to private business calculations and the principle that 'the polluter pays' has been hard to enforce on private owners of plants in one country without world-wide agreement and commitment to enforcement in all countries. Decentralised public owners should be much more concerned with pollution, because it will be their environment that is suffering, but regulation on a regional and even international level will be required to control free riders.

The Alternative

These suggestions for an alternative way to both the centrally planned economy and the market economy are presented here to indicate that it is not utopian to think beyond the framework of capitalism and a 'third way' of some kind of 'humanised' capitalism. There are very real possibilities already being discussed for an alternative 'humanised' socialism. Some of them have even been applied here and there. Cooperative principles are operating in small-scale factories and in small-scale farmers' associations. Some of these are linked together in networks of the fair trade movement. The role of non-governmental, not-for-profit organisations is becoming everywhere more important in supplying many of the services which we rely on every day.

An alternative must provide for popular participation at every level where people want to be involved. And for this involvement to be meaningful, information about what is happening in the economy, and what the choices are, must be made widely available and intelligible. Thanks to the developments in information technology this has become perfectly possible. So has the intervention of popular opinion in the debates of local and national representatives. Local authorities in Canada

already broadcast their debates and provide time for listeners and viewers to challenge speakers and literally to air their views. Of course all depends on the neutrality of the programme editor, but this shows what could be done.

A computerised model of the Chilean economy was created by Stanford Beer for Allende's socialist government in 1973. This not only recorded the main movements in the economy for the government planners, but made the information available in simplified form continuously updated on visual TV display, not only in local and central government offices, trade unions and other popular organisations but in factories and offices, wherever facilities existed. The implications of different economic policies could be made clear and public opinion consulted in advance of decisions being taken.

Nobody can say with Mrs Thatcher, and now with Mr Blair, that there is no alternative. There is and it works. Of course, it will not be popular with the very rich whose power will be challenged, as it was by Allende in Chile. Allende was brought down by a military coup, in which he and thousands of others died and the brutal military dictatorship of General Pinochet was established, resulting in the exile of a million Chileans. It is an awful warning, and it is often said that Allende was elected by no more than 40% of the electorate – roughly the same proportion as every post-war British government. But it raises very sharply the question how it would be possible to move from where we are today to envisaging the introduction of an alternative to capitalism.

J.M.Keynes "Speculators may do no harm as bubbles on a steady stream of enterprise. But the position is serious when enterprise becomes the bubble on the whirlpool of speculation. When the capital development of a country becomes a byproduct of the activities of a casino, the job is likely to be ill-done."

CHAPTER 10

Getting Out of the Crisis

Intermediate remedies and a long-term alternative vision provide a basic set of ideas for checking any worsening of the current crisis and avoiding future crises, but they do not get us out of the current mess. The G7 Finance Ministers representing the seven richest nations have met and promised to work together to stabilise the situation. But the sole policy on offer is that they should lower interest rates, and then not as a common policy but as each government thinks best. They have guaranteed the IMF a sum of $90 billions for rescue packages, but much of that is payments of contributions that are in arrears. Nonetheless, this must appear a very large sum, and in relation to the IMF's credit and loans outstanding of some $60 billions it is. But it needs to be set against the size of the emergency package of funds just negotiated by the Brazilian government with international institutions and governments to cover its debts. This package just for one country was worth between $30 and $40 billions, and proved not to be enough.

Who Benefits from Rescue Packages?

All countries hold a reserve of gold and hard currencies (i.e. ones that can be used anywhere) in order to tide them over deficits in their foreign balance of payments. The total reserves of all countries amount today to some $1500 billions, which is equal on average to about 4 months of world trade. Fifty years ago reserves were equal on average to about a year's world imports. This was reduced to the level of about 4 months by the 1970s, but then the IMF support was correspondingly much greater. Only the larger countries have reserves of that amount or over; the smaller ones are much more exposed. The architects of the Bretton Woods agreement had in mind much larger sums to fend off the kind of crisis that hit the world in 1929; but governments, and especially the United States government, which should supply about a fifth of all the IMF's funds, are generally well in arrears on their contributions.

There has been much talk of the comparative scale of Marshall Aid to Europe after 1948 and of the need to provide something similar for Russia in its present crisis. At today's prices Marshall Aid provided in 1948 alone a sum of grants well in excess of $100 billion. Russia has not received half as much as this even in loans. And, whereas Marshall Aid spending was left largely to the Europeans to determine as they thought best, the financial packages for Russia were tied to policies which we have already seen proved quite disastrous. Opening up the country to world financial movements encouraged wildly speculative investment in the country and a villainous flight of capital out of the country, when things began to go wrong.

The main objection to the packages being proposed by the G7 for halting the slide into slump is that they are designed to rescue the banks and other investors who have got their fingers burnt. Rather than the investors in the rich countries being made to pay for their errors or their greed, it is the poor in the poor countries who will pay, as their government expenditure is cut back in order to repay the borrowed monies and the interest due. No jobs will necessarily be saved or new jobs created as the result of such rescue packages. The Mexican rescue package in 1995, which is widely quoted as a model, left rich income taxpayers almost untouched, but the standard of living of average Mexicans was sharply cut back. It had not grown for a decade and the poor had already become successively poorer.

How to Create Jobs in a Crisis

Job creation in times of general economic growth requires some quite small government intervention to ensure that, alongside private investment that is likely to be labour saving, there is an element of public investment in labour-intensive activities. If there is a real slide in employment into a slump, something more is needed. Each individual government can step up its public spending to halt the rise in unemployment. This is likely to be much more effective than having to increase payments to the unemployed. There will be screams from industry that their dogma tells them that increased public spending is at the expense of private consumption. The industrialists need to be told that such public spending will on the contrary step up demand for their products.

Even the Bank of England has admitted that there is no danger now of inflation. It is continued growth that is in question. **What is now needed is that a programme of national renewal should be undertaken – to create jobs, especially in areas of industrial decline, but specifically in order to correct some of the many environmentally destructive effects of industrial development in the last decades.** It is not enough to say that the polluter will pay. The state will have to take over much of the cleaning up that has been left to be done after 50 years of ill-regulated economic growth. Such work is very labour-intensive and could take up some sections of the unemployed. It is not by any means all unskilled manual work. Recycling and modern waste disposal techniques require technical skills and some training in the natural sciences.

Such a rescue and renewal programme can take advantage of the relative strength of the British economy. But tackling such problems cannot be undertaken solely on the level of the nation state. If it is, other countries with no such programmes will take advantage of the state spending and increase their sales in the new markets created, as free riders at the expense of the British producers. **The obvious answer is to launch a European Recovery Programme**. This was the official title of the Marshall Plan for US aid to post-war Europe in 1947. It needs to be revived, but the funds can now be found from within Europe, by mobilising the very considerable savings that have been generated in a period of prosperity for the more affluent.

For entry into the European Economic and Monetary Union, all aspirants for membership have been bringing their state spending and borrowing under control according to the guidelines laid down in the Maastricht Treaty. These guidelines need not necessarily be breached, as we suggested earlier, if all member states agree on common action through the European Investment Fund and for issuing Euro-bonds. There are already on the table the Delors proposals for such all-European investment in transport, medium and small enterprise assistance and regional development, which are awaiting authorisation up to a figure of some 60 billion ecus (about $70 billion). Euro-bonds, if they were to be issued, could more than double that figure as President Mitterrand once proposed.

A New Political Leadership in Europe

Authorisation has been held up so far by the Finance Ministers (meeting as ECOFIN) who have assumed that there will be a strong inflationary effect of such spending and whose governments have feared the federal implications of such large expenditures outside national budgets. The political complexion of the three largest states in Europe has changed in the last two years, so that we have Socialist (France), Social Democrat/Green (Germany) and Labour (UK) governments of the Centre-Left in place of governments of the Right. In addition the Italian government generally has left-wing support, and currently a 'Communist' Prime Minister, and there are several governments of the smaller countries with a left of centre

Dominique Strauss-Kahn (top left), Oskar Lafontaine (top right), Mario Monti (bottom left) and Gordon Brown (bottom right)

orientation. Even Mr Brown has joined in rather belatedly calling for the bankers to emphasise employment as well as price stability.

If this is not a moment for common action to demonstrate the concern of the Left for the unemployed, and to recognise the danger of further unemployment and damage to the environment, it is hard to imagine when there would be such a moment. Herr Lafontaine, as German Finance Minister, along with his French counterpart, M. Strauss-Kahn, showed the way in taking up once more the Delors proposals and placing them before the Euro summit at Vienna in late 1998. They were immediately and sharply reprimanded by the German Central Bank Chairman and by the new President of the European Central Bank. This is a tug-of-war, which Lafontaine has temporarily lost.

Box 34. The Dream World of ECOFIN

'We are reaping the rewards of stability orientation in the form of budgetary adjustment and declining inflation... the European Union is conspicuous as a pole of stability conducive to economic and employment growth... Solutions [to problems] depend on national and political situations.'

Quoted by Philip Stephens, 'Basking in Myopia', *Financial Times*, 28. 9.98

Up till the Vienna meeting, the only concession to the concept of common action to solve problems, including unemployment and the failure of economic growth, was the agreement of governments in 1997 to draw up National Action Plans following certain European Employment Policy Guidelines. These came to nothing, because there was no requirement to meet specific measurable targets for reducing unemployment rates and for increasing employment, nor any clear indications of how this might be done, and what the implications might be for national budgets and European Union finances. Now that the French and German governments have changed, the details of possible common action become important.

The European Union is not only one of the wealthiest regions in the world, it has a tradition of social regulation and complex democratic institutions. Historically, it is the home of socialist thought and experiment.

For a long time this was usurped by the brutal dictatorship of Stalin and almost destroyed by the Nazi terror. Recovery since the Second World War has, furthermore, been overlaid by the hegemonic power of the United States and the Atlantic Alliance. The revival of socialist leadership in France and Germany and in Italy, combined with social democratic traditions in the smaller European countries, makes possible the extrication of British Labour from the American embrace and all it has meant in financial and military domination throughout the post-war years.

Detailed Proposals for Job Creation

Box 35. Proposed Employment Policy Guidelines for 1999

- Halving the unemployment rate of each Member State within five years, with intermediate targets for each year
- At least 50% of unemployed in active measures of training
- Employment guarantees for young unemployed and long term unemployed of at least one year after training
- Guaranteed right of two years of paid further education or training to all over 25 years of age
- Reduction of maximum weekly working hours to 40 hours in 5 years and promotion of 35/30 hour week and flexibility of working hours
- Promotion of job rotation schemes to integrate long-term unemployed into the first labour market
- Promotion of equal opportunities with quotas for women, guaranteed child care facilities, etc.
- Promotion of work for elderly and disabled persons
- Clear and full statement of national budgetary implication of strengthening public sector activity
- Reducing the VAT rate for labour-intensive production and services oriented to internal demand
- Extending fiscal federalism, through reform of the structural funds to promote investment in health, education, urban renewal, environment, culture, and public non-commercial electronic networks
- Reserving one third of the structural funds for local development and local initiatives
- In order to finance a European common programme of employment generation, pooling of the Central Banks' reserves, not needed by the European Central Bank ($90-100 billion), authorising the agreed investment proposals for the European Investment Fund, except for the ecologically unacceptable TEN projects, and introducing EUROBONDS to finance specific European-wide employment projects.

Summarised from a paper by Frieder Otto Wolf, MEP, German Greens
In Ken Coates, MEP, *et al. Full Employment: A European Appeal*, Spokesman, 1998

How to Pay

In earlier chapters, we have suggested that richer households will have to be taxed more if greater equality and economic stability is to be achieved. But it was there recognised that this would imply a considerable educational task by government to overcome the selfish individualism that is the legacy of the Thatcher-Reagan years. A beginning could undoubtedly be made with taxes that were hypothecated like National

Insurance, for specific purposes – education, health, environmental protection etc. A further windfall tax on the profits of the privatised public utilities could be introduced as an emergency measure to take some of the cream off the 'fat cats', since this tax was a one-off and its aim – to get young people and long term unemployed off welfare and into work – has not yet been accomplished.

An alternative would be to make major savings on military spending. Although these could not be realised for several years, the impact could begin to affect employment as the switch was made from military to civilian spending. The reason for this is that military spending is highly capital-intensive. Nuclear submarines, aircraft carriers and fighter-bombers today include large quantities of equipment which is produced by automation and quite small amounts of labour, even though some may be highly skilled. By contrast most civilian spending, on education and health for example, includes quite small amounts of equipment and great quantities of labour, much of it professional.

The sums involved are very large. Scrapping the Trident would yield £1 billion a year for some years. The planned building of two new aircraft carriers will cost £8 billion over about 8 years. The 232 new Eurofighters are to cost £16 billions over ten years. Reducing British 'defence' spending to the average level in the European Union would raise

£6 billions a year. Withdrawing British troops from Germany would save £2 billions a year. We are talking about savings on military expenditure of some £12 billions a year. This could be used for projects which would create about twice as many jobs as were lost. If the net cost of creating one new job is £10,000, something over half a million new jobs could be created.

When the Cold War ended, it was hoped that there would be a peace dividend from the savings on arms expenditure. It hasn't happened. Many firms have continued to produce arms, and have been busily finding foreign wars where they could be sold to the combatants – on either side.

Governments, moreover, have been happy to reduce their total expenditure, as they reduced their arms spending. This can be seen as another cause of declining employment, particularly in those parts of the country where ship-building and heavy engineering were concentrated. Reversing the trend is not going to be easy, but, as the unemployment figures rise, pressure for increased public spending can be expected to grow.

The other likely development in a period of rising unemployment is the pressure of those threatened with unemployment for an all-round reduction in hours of work. When we studied proposals for shortening the working year in an earlier chapter (chapter 8), we recognised that it would necessarily be a long business to create any large number of new jobs. But no other way could be more effective in the longer run.

To make a start now with the aim of increasing the number of job opportunities would imply a considerable input of government compensation for loss of earnings for workers working shorter hours, since there would be little time for employers to make the improvements in productivity necessary to adapt to shorter hours of work. Governments could finance this compensation from unemployment funds where they could establish that new jobs had actually been created by work sharing and similar schemes.

World-wide Action

Not all the suggestions listed above will receive universal support, even on the Left, but they indicate the two main pillars for creating jobs: the reduction in working time and the development of the public sector. What they do not include is an extra-European element. The myopia revealed by the European Finance Ministers blinded them to the reciprocal benefits to be derived from expanded trade, not only with Eastern Europe but also with the Third World. This, as we have seen, means support for commodity producers and now for Asian industries.

We have seen earlier the double standards in the matter of protecting national industries – the North preaching to the South the necessity for free trade, while at the same time protecting its agriculture, textiles and electronics industries. The argument for Europe to open its markets to Asian products, with proper controls over dumping goods at prices below their own home prices, is not just a matter of fairness, but of general advantage. Consumers in the North will benefit and, provided that those who control production in the North make the necessary changes in what they produce, the Asians too will benefit from widening markets.

Box 36. Double Standards in Banking

'How can the Fed. [the United States central bank) justify "asking" leading banks in the world to bail out *Long Term Capital Management* when all the while the mantra of "accountability", "transparency", "prudent lending" and "free market" is being prescribed and forced upon Asian countries. We in Asia are being told that we "must" let bad companies and banks that borrow or lend excessively go under, and that it is a good thing for the economy. We were told not to bail out any companies as this would be seen as interfering with market forces and will only prolong and delay the adjustment of the "real" economy.

How can LTCM's high stake gambling of $200 billion in the stock market be justified and the bank lending to it be termed prudent lending? How can it be that it is crony capitalism when an Asian government helps viable companies that provide jobs and incomes to millions of people to be self-reliant, yet it is not crony capitalism when the US bails out LTCM and a few millionaires along the way?'

Frederick Wong, Letter to the *Financial Times*, 5.10.98

The only advantage to either North or South from the raising of protective barriers is for the less developed to catch up with the more developed. For Southern producers their only hope of development is by having access to world markets. Protection in the North just serves to reduce the whole level of world trade. Those who argue for protection for the already industrialised countries are either demanding a short-term advantage for producers (often paid for by someone else as in the case of the taxpayers paying to subsidise agriculture in the North), which has long run disadvantages, or they believe that we could all live better without the wide range of goods that international trade provides.

What is Now Most Needed: A Change of Ideas

None of the proposals discussed here will be realised unless a successful onslaught is mobilised against the theoretical underpinnings of the whole monetarist philosophy which dominates the current thinking of bankers, industrialists and governments alike. Owners of capital will always do all they can to protect their money, and short-term arguments may well attract them because their active lives are short. But the present crisis is spreading ruin among many who imagined they were immune.

The central contradiction of capitalism, which we have already revealed, is that **the very attempt on a wide scale to increase the returns to capital reduces the possibility of realising the sales from capital investment**. Professor Brenner's study of the last 50 years showed that the more that the power of capital was strengthened over the power of labour, the less well did the system perform.

Today's crisis is its nemesis. Of course, capitalism might still recover after a slump of similar proportions to that of the 1930s, but we have to remember what happened between then and subsequent recovery – the rise of fascism, the holocaust, the gulag and a world war of devastating destructiveness. Today, with nuclear weapons arsenals in many hands, humanity just dare not afford such a repetition.

The seriousness of the current crisis undoubtedly has the bankers exposed as both greedy and reckless. It would be a mistake to draw the conclusion which Mr Blair has drawn that they must simply be made to operate in a more transparent fashion and subject to greater independent regulation. **The problem lies in the system they are operating which makes them greedy and reckless. That is the very nature of the competitive world of capital accumulation.** Criticisms of the working of the capitalist system are being made on all sides every day now, that would have been unheard of a few months ago.

Those who have always argued for an alternative economic system cannot let the moment pass to press the case for an alternative. There is not likely to be any automatic revolutionary change just because the slump

becomes a deep one. On past experience it is reactionary forces that benefit from economic collapse and not progress. The greatest human advances in the last two centuries have been made in periods of relative peace – according to the UNDP studies of human development – in the years after 1850, and again in the 1950s and 60s. But wars and disorders had the effect of shaking up people's ideas and particularly their certainties about the social order.

The chief lesson that the current crisis must teach us is that competition is not the most effective way of conducting the economy. Human beings have survived through the combination of competitiveness *and* cooperation. In harsher tropical and arctic conditions, the cooperative instinct, exhibited most particularly among the women, has been necessary for survival. In more benign temperate climes, the competitive spirit has been given free rein, encouraging the most extraordinary development of human competitive inventiveness to the point where we stand on the edge of an ecological disaster. The downgrading of the female role in this development needs urgently to be reversed if we are to survive – that is to say, not women competing like men, but exhibiting all the capacity for cooperation that they are born with.

As a first step it is essential that the governments of Europe, not least the British, should begin to educate their electors in the importance of cooperation – first in Europe and then world-wide in correcting the ruinous policies that the bankers have been pursuing. It is fear of the bankers that has made so many people hesitate in their support for closer working together in the European Union, since it has been presented as a monetary union to be managed by an unaccountable European Central Bank. But the new political alignments in Europe can put the bankers in their place and ensure that popular policies of full employment, social provision and environmental protection are restored.

If public opinion began to recognise the urgent need for European governments' cooperation to create employment and rescue the environment, and so to offset the power of the bankers and the transnational corporations, even Mr Murdoch would see that, to keep his readers, he would have to follow their new sentiments; and in the face of a pending world slump European governments would have to modify the Maastricht Treaty to allow them to take common measures at once to prevent the slump from deepening and continuing.

With the emergence of new Centre-Left governments in Germany France and Italy, at a time of serious economic crisis, it may still be possible to extricate the New Labour Government in Britain from its obsession with the failed economic orthodoxies of neo-classical Monetarism. There is nothing like changing realities to bring about a change in ideas.

Business can help to change the world for the better. **Liza Ramrayka** looks at some examples which have challenged conventional thinking and could be eligible for a new award

Fair enough

Ethical consumers with a sweet tooth and farmers in Ghana both stand to benefit from the recent launch of a chocolate bar made from fairly-traded cocoa beans. Called Divine, the bar is the latest initiative from Twin Trading, a not-for-profit organisation working with small-scale farmers in developing countries to ensure they get fair prices from Western buyers.

Divine, which is being stocked by retailers including Tesco and the Co-op, is produced from beans supplied by Kuapa Kokoo, a Ghanaian cocoa-growers collective which has a one-third stake in the project. It is just the kind of initiative which will be the focus of a new award scheme, co-sponsored by the Guardian, the Directory of Social Change and the NatWest banking group, aiming to honour not-for-profit organisations that use commercial activities to address social issues.

Twin Trading, founded in 1985 by the GLC, supports producers through business advice and training, trading and the development of distribution chains. The company's charitable arm is the driving force behind fair-trade coffee brand Cafédirect, and is also involved in sourcing fairly-traded goods for the Body Shop and Oxfam Trading.

Twin Trading's staff of 20 includes small business advisors, agronomists and information workers. The company last year had a turnover of £4 million, working with farmers from Costa Rica to Cameroon to trade a range of goods including peanuts and bananas.

Pauline Tiffen, Twin Trade's director, says the company acts as an "alternative merchant" which empowers producers to compete in global markets. "It's usually the poorest people producing these commodities, so we help to bring them to the market in a way that they won't get ripped off."

Tiffen says this approach fosters self-sufficiency in Twin Trading's producer partners. "We are not an aid agency; we help them to trade viably and to have a future."

One of the most high-profile examples of an organisation addressing social objectives through commercial means is the Big Issue. Set up in 1991 with funding from the Body Shop, the magazine is sold by homeless and insecurely-housed people who keep 60p of the £1 cover price. There are now five editions of the magazine for different parts of the UK, with a total of 300,000 copies sold each week. Each one passes part of its profits to a separate charitable trust, which helps those selling the magazine to re-settle.

The Big Issue in the North Trust, now two years old, is the charitable arm of the organisation's operation across Manchester, Liverpool and Leeds. The trust recently introduced a range of additional services at its Manchester office, including an employment unit, IT training suite and doctor's surgery. Val Chinn, its chief executive, says the commercial element of the organisation is an essential part of its vision. "Selling the magazine is easy-access employment for people who would otherwise be excluded from work. And profits that come back to us can then help support vendors as part of their long-term resettlement programme."

While Twin Trading and the Big Issue have had several years' experience of what many call "social business", other organisations are just dipping a toe in the water. Praxis, an east London charity set up in 1983, provides free advice and training for the 250,000 refugees and asylum-seekers

Toby Peters

Box 37. Defunct Ideas

'the ideas of economists and political philosophers, both when they are right and when they are wrong, are more powerful than is commonly understood. Indeed the world is ruled by little else. Practical men, who believe themselves to be quite exempt from any intellectual influences, are usually the slaves of some defunct economists. Madmen in authority, who hear voices in the air, are distilling their frenzy from some academic scribbler of a few years back.'

John Maynard Keynes, *The General Theory of Employment, Interest and Money*, 1936

The Monetarist academic scribblers have had their day. It is time we put an end to their influence and the financial gambling which they have encouraged, so that we may have the confidence to begin to rebuild the real economy of jobs and food, housing and health, education and creative leisure which they have put at risk. This is a practical task, but it requires new ways of thinking to sustain it.

This little book is offered as a contribution to a new and better understanding of the way the real economy works and of what has to be done to make it work not just better in the old way, but actually in a new and more just way. It will only be possible to achieve such a better state of affairs if we both understand what has to be done and find ways of working together to make it happen. Changes of the kind proposed in this book will not come from the top downward. New political leaders committed to creating full employment and a more equal and just society are to be welcomed, but their effectiveness will depend entirely on the social movement carrying them forward. This movement consists of a very wide range of separate forces – trade unions, organisations of the unemployed, feminists, greens, old age pensioners' associations, student bodies and campaigning groups of all sorts, for world peace, better and more comprehensive schooling, a truly universal health service, improved housing, public transport, fair trade and debt relief for poor peoples. Working together in alliance they would be invincible.

It is the great challenge of our time to build that alliance – not just in our own country but world-wide.

world music ethical shopping world food
OLYMPIA 2 DECEMBER 11TH 12TH 13TH
NEXT TO KENSINGTON (OLYMPIA) TUBE STATION
11am – 7pm Fri/Sat
11am – 5pm Sunday
£5 (incl. handbook), Conc. £2.50, Family (2+2) £10
The fair trade fair
Full programme in The Big Issue 30th November
If you would like more information about any aspect of the programme, or if you can help on the day, or distribute leaflets to friends, colleagues and contacts, please send SAE to PO BOX 1007 London SE24 9NL. E-mail: globalpartnership@yahoo.com
Global Partnership '98

References and Further Reading

Abel Aganbegyan, *The Challenge: The Economics of Perestroika*, Hutchinson, 1988

Michael Barratt Brown, *Models in Political Economy*, Penguin Books, 1995

Defending the Welfare State, Independent Labour Network, 1998

Michael Barratt Brown & Ken Coates, MEP, *The Blair Revelation*, Spokesman, 1996

Michael Barratt Brown & Hugo Radice, *Democracy versus Capitalism: A Reply to Will Hutton*, Spokesman, 1996

Tony Blair, *The Third Way: New Politics for the New Century*, Fabian Society, September 1998

Robert Brennan, *The Economics of Global Turbulence*, New Left Review, No. 229, May-June, 1998

Noam Chomsky, 'Power in the Global Arena', *New Left Review*, no.230, July-Aug., 1998

David Coates & John Hillard, *UK Economic Decline: Key Texts*, Harvester, 1995

Ken Coates and Stuart Holland, *Full Employment for Europe*, Spokesman, 1995

Ken Coates MEP *et al., Full Employment: A European Appeal*, Spokesman, 1998

W. Paul Cockshott & Allin Cottrell, *Towards a New Socialism*, Spokesman, 1993

J.K. Galbraith, *The Culture of Contentment*, Mandarin 1995

J.K. Galbraith, *The Great Crash, 1929*, Pelican 1956

Anthony Giddens, *The Third Way*, Polity Press, 1998

Stuart Holland, *The European Imperative*, Spokesman, 1993

Will Hutton, *The State We're In*, Jonathan Cape, 1995

John Mills, *Tackling Britain's False Economy*, Macmillan, 1997

Peter Lang, *LETS Work: Rebuilding the Local Economy*, Grover Books, 1994

Jonathan Perraton *et al.*, 'The Globalisation of Economic Activity', *New Political Economy*, vol.2, no.2, 1997

Jonathan Porritt (ed.), *The Real World*, Kogan Page, 1996

Joseph Schumpeter, *Business Cycles*, McGraw Hill, 1951

George Soros, *The Crisis of Capitalism*, Little Brown, 1998

UNDP, *Human Development Report 1997*, New York, 1997

Human Development Report 1998, New York, 1998

Glossary and Acronyms

Accumulation – of capital, by continued interest
Algorithm – rules for computer calculation
Assets – any possession that can be used to meet debts
Barter – exchange of goods or services without money
Billion – 1000 million
Biome – a community of fauna or flora adapted to a particular location
Bond – promise to repay borrowed money at a fixed rate and time
Brand – exclusive trade name of particular make of goods
Bretton Woods – place in the USA of founding in 1944 of the international financial institutions – IMF and World Bank
Capacity – the output of which a plant is capable
Capital – money for accumulation, used in business for extended activity
  controls – regulation by governments of capital movement
  -to-Labour ratio – proportions of each applied to any business
  – intensive – using much capital per unit of output
Capitalization – money converted into capital
Central Bank – the Government owned or controlled bank in any country, which controls the issue of money
Command economy – where the market is replaced by government dictation
Credit – power to obtain goods before payment on promise to pay later
Creditor – someone to whom money is owed by a person or company
Currency – money in use in any country
  Hard currency, one that like the dollar is convertible into others
  Reserve – that can be used to pay foreign debts, e.g. dollars
Debt – generally what a country's owes to foreign governments, banks etc.
Deficit – excess of liabilities over assets of persons, companies or governments
Deflation – reduction by government of money/activity in the economy
Demand – volume of decisions at any time to purchase goods or services
De-regulation – reduction of government controls, e.g. over the use of labour
Devaluation – reduction of a currency's value in relation to other currencies
Emerging economies – those which were under Communist Party rule
Equity – the value of a share in the ownership of a company
Exposure – openness to risk of financial loss
Eurobond – bonds issued by the European Union
Eurodollar – dollar used in trade outside the USA
Financial institutions – banks, insurance companies etc. dealing in money
Fiscal policy – government taxing and spending
Franchise – right granted by a manufacturer or distributor to sell products
Funds – money set aside, e.g. for paying interest
Futures – commodities including money bought or sold at an agreed price for delivery at a later date
Gearing – ratio of equity to fixed interest borrowings
Haven – safe place to leave money, e.g. offshore, to avoid local taxation
Hedge – counterbalance one transaction with another to avoid risk
  fund – for buying now (spot) and selling later (futures) or the other way round, to avoid risk of price changes
Income – personal or company earnings over a period, e.g. a year
  tax – direct claim of government on % of annual earnings
  Unearned – personal income from savings, investments etc
Incomes Policy – government controls over wages and salary payments
Indirect taxes – those paid with the purchase, e.g. VAT, customs & excise
Inflation – continuing rise in retail prices and fall in the value of money
  rate – at a certain rate per year
Infrastructure – a country's roads, bridges, sewers, water and power supply
Keynesian – economic ideas of J.M.Keynes concerned with government maintaining effective demand in the economy
Labour – the human factor in production
  flexibility – variability in labour time
  force – all the workers in a plant or country
  saving – using less labour on production
  value – measure of value in terms of labour
  intensive – using much labour per unit of output
Lender – supplier of money, generally at interest
  Of Last Resort – a central government bank, the bankers' bank
Leverage – see gearing, the increase of the fixed interest proportion
Liberalisation – freeing business, finance from government controls
Liquidity – having assets in cash sufficient to meet all debts
Liquidation – winding up the affairs of a company, paying off creditors
Macro-economics – concerned with the big things, state policy etc.
Market – place where exchanges take place e.g.

Stock Exchange and Job Centre
Micro-economics – concerned with the small things, firms etc.
Monetarism – belief in government control of the money supply to stop inflation as the most important government task
Monopoly – literally the power of a single producer or seller, used for any exercise of large and exclusive power in a market
Multi-national companies – those that have owners in several countries
Neo-classical – school of economics emphasising mathematical analysis of small changes, e.g. in prices
Network – a system of intersecting lines of communication, especially for decentralising business activities
Productivity – of labour, the output of a plant or company measured in relation to labour input
  increase, the annual rate of growth of output per labour input
Profit – the return on a business investment after all expenses are paid, to be used to pay share-holders or for investment in future development
  rate – the percentage return to capital invested over a period, e.g. a year
Protection – measures taken by governments to control imports of goods or services competing with those produced locally
Rationalisation – reorganisation of a firm or other enteprise to reduce costs
Reform – any correction of error or abuse, but now used to describe changes in Government policies to open the economy to the market
Reserves – government holdings of gold or hard currency, with which to pay for imports if these exceed exports or to pay off foreign debts
Speculation – sale or purchase in any market not for use but solely to make money on what may be a risky gamble
Stock exchange – a place where stocks and shares in governments and companies are bought and sold and their prices made
Structural adjustment – changes in government policies to open economies to world markets, i.e. for foreign goods and capital
Subsidiarity – the concept, especially popular in the European Union, of delegating as much as possible to a lower level, e.g. national
Subsidy – a payment generally by government to make a sale or purchase by a person or company profitable, and so keep them in busines
Supply side – the side of the schedule of demand and supply in the market, especially for labour, which reflects the quantity and quality of labour available and the conditions attached to it
Surplus – any excess of income over expenditure, e.g. on government accounts or a country's foreign trade balance
Taxation – government levies on persons, companies and goods and services
  Direct – on the income of persons and companies
  Indirect – on sales, VAT etc
Technology – application of inventions/science to industry and commerce
Tele-working – use of computer and E Mail for distance reading/writing
Third World – name given to countries that were once colonies of European Empires and are now very poor
Trade (foreign)– exchanges between countries
  Free – without government controls such as tariffs and quotas
  cycles – the booms and slumps in economic activity
Transfer pricing – the valuation of exchanges inside companies operating in different countries, often to avoid tax
Transnational companies – those that operate in several countries
Trillion – a million million
War economy – one based on total government control of resources

ACRONYMS

ECB – European Central Bank
ECOFIN – European Council of Finance Ministers
EMU – European Economic and Monetary Union
EU – European Union
FED – United States Federal Reserve Bank
GATT – General Agreement on Tariffs and Trade
GEF – General Environmental Fund
GDP – Gross Domestic Product
G 7 – the meeting of the top leaders of the seven richest states
IDA – International Development Agency
ILO – International Labour Office
IMF – International Monetary Fund
Kondratieff – long (50 year) trade cycle
Maastricht – Treaty of EU on preparation for EMU
MAI – Multilateral Agreement on Investment
MEP – Member of the European Parliament
MNC – Multi-national Company
NAIRU – Non-accelerating Inflation Rate of Unemployment
NGO – Non-Governmental Organisation
OECD – Organisation for Economic Cooperation and Development
OPEC – Organisation of Petroleum Exporting Countries
SME – Small and Medium-sized Companies
TNC – Trans-national Company
TUC – Trade Union Congress
UNCTAD – United Nations Conference on Trade and Development
UNDP – United Nations Development Programme
UNESCO – United Nations Education, Science and Cultural Organisation
UNICEF – United Nations International Children's Emergency Fund
UNPFA – United Nations Population Fund
WB – World Bank
WTO – World Trade Organisation

Sources of Illustrations

The cartoons except Steve Bell's are taken from Michael Barratt Brown, *Information at Work*, Hutchinson, 1979

Page

Cover UNDP *Human Development Report* 1998 and *Financial Times* Mexico Supplement 1998

x *Financial Times*, 6.10.98

xi *Economist*, 12.9.98

xiii *Wired*, November 1997 article by the editor

4 *Guardian G2*, Rory Caroll story, 28.10.98

5 Fernand Braudel, *Civilisation and Capitalism*, vol. 1., and picture in *Financial Times*, 21.10.98

7 Readers Digest, *Life in the 20s and 30s*

10 *Financial Times*, 21.10.98

11 Braudel, *op.cit.*

14 Michael Barratt Brown *Information at Work*

15 *Guardian*, 18.11.98

17 Larry Elliott, *Guardian*, 17.11.98

18 *Voice of the Unions*, November 1998

20 *Economist*, 14.11.98

23 Sean Sprague (*Panos*) on cover of Ben Jackson *Poverty and the Planet*, Penquin

25 *Financial Times*, 23.9.98

27 *Economist*, 9.1.9

28 Readers Digest, *op.cit.*

29 John Wells, *European Labour Forum*, no. 13, Summer 1994

30 BP *Report* for 1986

31 Monopolies and Mergers Commission

33 Helen Bradley, *Going Home through the Snow*, Bridgeman Art Library

35 Cover of Penguin edition of Marx's *Capital* vol.1

37 Joshua S. Goldstein, *Long Cycles, Yale University Press: New Haven and London*

41 Michael Barratt Brown, taken from the European Commission, *European Economy Annual Economic Report for 1997.*

45 Larry Elliott, *Guardian*, 11.11.98

47 UNDP, *Human Development Report 1998*

49 Michael Barratt Brown, *Defending the Welfare State*, Spokesman, 1997

50 *Financial Times*

53 *Financial Times*, 17.8.98

55 *European Labour Forum*, no. 12

57 Michael Barratt Brown and Ken Coates MEP, *Community Under Attack*, Spokesman, fig. 1

59 *Guardian*, 4.11.98

61 *Guardian*, **OR** (Belinda Corte, *The Trade Trap*, Oxfam)

62 Michael Barratt Brown, cover of *Morphology of Debt*, Spokesman, 1997

63 Michael Barratt Brown, *Fair Trade*, Zed Press, 1993

65 *Economist*, 3.10.98, p.21

66 *International Labour Reports*, no. 40, 1990

69 *European Labour Forum*, no. 19, 1997

71 New Internationalist, *World Guide 1997-9*

73 *European Labour Forum*, cover, no. 18, 1996-7

75 ditto

76 ditto, cover, no. 10, 1992

78 Michael Barratt Brown, *Fair Trade*, *op.cit.*

79 Asa Briggs, *Social History of England*, Weidenfield, p.267

82 *Financial Times*, 4.11.98

84 Lance Taylor, "Capital Market Crisis", *Cambridge Journal of Economics*, 1998 vol.22

86 Clause IV from a Labour Party card, prior to 1996

87 Michael Barratt Brown, *Models in Political Economy*, revised ed. 1995, p.385

89 *The Guardian*, Editor, 28.11.98

89 *The Guardian*, 2.10.98

93 *Financial Times*, 9.12.98

94 *European Labour Forum*, cover, no. 20, 1998-9

96 Steve Bell, *Guardian*, 15.1.98

101 *The Guardian*

103 Fair Trade Fair advert, Christmas 1998